I0039813

Condo Board Election Revolt!

Condo Board Election Revolt!

How Florida's First Condo Ombudsman Became the 500-Pound Gorilla

Valmore R. Lucier

A Condo Commandos 101 Reality Book
Publisher: Dr. Joyce Starr
Imprint: Little Guy Pawprint
www.DrJoyceStarr.com

Publisher: Dr. Joyce Starr
Imprint: Little Guy Pawprint
A Condo Commandos 101 Reality Book
www.DrJoyceStarr.com
Aventura, Florida

© 2006 by Valmore R. Lucier. All Rights Reserved.

Published in the United States of America

No part of this book may be used or reproduced, stored in a retrieval system, or transmitted in any form or by any means, electronic, mechanical, photocopying, recording or otherwise, except in the case of brief quotations embodied in articles or reviews and as permitted under Section 107 or 108 of the 1976 United States Copyright Act, without the prior permission of the publisher.

ISBN 978-0-9792333-9-5

This book is available for special promotions. Please contact: info@DrJoyceStarr.com

First Edition – 2007

Printed in the United States of America.

From the Publisher

Our small publishing house is designed to work closely with writers who have empowering and inspirational material to share.

Publishing is perceived as an impersonal process. Yet the publisher and senior editor often have more intense contact with the author and a deeper involvement in the author's project than most readers.

The publisher received this work the first week of December 2006, along with an urgent request that it be produced in soft-cover format by the third week of January 2007. We were also asked to refine the draft document for clarity of content.

There were two goals. First, to put this work in the hands of key Florida legislators before they began writing new laws for the 2007 Session. Second, to help frame legislation for condo board elections that would improve the lives of condo owners in Florida and across the nation.

This was a challenging task given the sensitive nature of the material and the brief holiday time frame. Nevertheless, the target deadline was met. We hope the author's message will be widely disseminated to those who can make a difference – including condo association boards.

Disclaimer

While the publisher and author have used their best efforts in preparing this book, they make no representation or warranties with respect to the accuracy or completeness of the contents of this book and specifically disclaim any implied warranties of merchantability or fitness for a particular purpose. No warranty may be created or extended by sales representatives or written sales materials. The advice and strategies contained herein may not be suitable for your situation. The publisher is not engaged in rendering professional services, and you should consult with a professional where appropriate. Neither the publisher nor the author shall be liable for any loss of profit or any other commercial damages, including but not limited to special, incidental, consequential or other damages.

"I am only one, but still I am one; I cannot do everything; but I can do something; and because I cannot do everything; I will not refuse to do something that I can do."

Edward Everett Hale

Dedication

To my wife Doris and my son Ron without whose encouragement this effort would not have been started.

And to Virgil and all of the dedicated Volunteer Election Monitors.

Acknowledgments

No man is an island onto himself, especially when writing a book. There are many collaborators, each contributing in his or her own way to the success of the endeavor. Many thanks are in order.

To my wife Doris, without whose encouragement this effort would not have been started or might even have been abandoned, and for the many reheated meals, nights spent alone, cancelled outings... and for absorbing my house chores so that I could concentrate on this effort.

To Connie Young, who hung in there with me from the very start, for always responding in a timely manner to my writing needs, taking less than 24 hours off for surgery, and for working long hours well into the night to glue all of my pieces into a finished product.

To Virgil Rizzo, for taking time off from his medical recovery to perform a technical review of my completed manuscript.

To Representative Julio Robaina, for finding time in his busy schedule to read my manuscript and graciously write the foreword to the book.

To my publisher and editor Dr. Joyce Starr, for untold hours transforming my manuscript into an effective and cohesive message, preparing it for publication and creating the final cover design.

To graphics artists Jonathan D. and Polette Villalta, for rendering powerful cover artwork.

To Jan Bergemann, for having confidence in the project and orchestrating the entire effort.

To all the volunteer monitor for making the program so successful. Without them there would not have been a monitor program.

And finally to all the readers who had the interest and the desire to read the book. To all of you I offer a heart felt

Thank You!

– Valmore R. Lucier

Table of Contents

Appendices

Foreword

Val Lucier's book is educational. It demonstrates how much more work must be undertaken to establish stringent legislative reforms that will be fair to condo owners. The integrity of elections in associations has been seriously compromised. Legislative intent calls for fair and democratic elections, not elections that pit condo boards against condo owners.

Even with competent condo election monitors in place, this work underscores why condo board elections so often prove detrimental to owners.

Integrity of elections will be accomplished only when legislative reforms ensure that condo owners have fair and democratic election procedures in place that are firmly enforced.

– Florida State Representative, Julio Robaina

Preface

How would you like to wake up tomorrow with a million and a half people looking to you for guidance and assistance? That's what happened to me when I was appointed the first Condominium Ombudsman for the State of Florida, and the first ever in the United States.

It was immediately apparent that this would be a daunting task. Among other priorities, the legislature mandated the Ombudsman to appoint election monitors to conduct elections of boards of directors in condominiums.

Although the legislature established guidelines, many aspects of the election process were left undefined. This placed a heavy burden on the Ombudsman to select people to serve as official monitors and to set standards and create uniformity in the election monitor process.

The experiences and escapades of the author of this book influenced the policies and procedures that are helping to prevent election misconduct, manipulation and controversy throughout the State of Florida.

**– Former Florida Condominium Ombudsman,
Dr. Virgil Rizzo**

Introduction

I served as the first Volunteer Chief Election Monitor in the office of the first Florida Ombudsman, Dr. Virgil Rizzo. I wrote this book for those interested in the inner workings of the Florida Condominium Election Monitor process. It contains information you could only receive from me or from Dr. Rizzo.

You will not find many names or places in this book. They have been left out intentionally to protect the innocent and to allow the guilty to remain anonymous. My hope is that this book will shed light on the very difficult and nearly impossible task that Dr. Virgil Rizzo so willingly undertook for Floridians.

On June 1, 2006, to all of our surprise, Governor Jeb Bush rescinded Dr. Virgil Rizzo's appointment as Condominium Ombudsman. In my opinion, Virgil's termination was based on totally erroneous allegations – to be revealed at the close of this book. Governor Jeb Bush did not discuss or otherwise confront Dr. Rizzo with these charges. In fact, amazing as it may be, the Governor never even met with Virgil. Instead, as a "reward" for Dr. Rizzo's tireless and dedicated service, a short termination notice was posted on the door of his apartment. An agency staff member left a voice message on his telephone. His State e-mail access was cut off and the lock on his office door was changed. A new Ombudsman was quickly appointed. Virgil's

1

Condo Board Election Revolt!

termination came on the heels of major back surgery and took place while he was still on medical leave – recuperating during a brief, but much deserved holiday cruise.

The State bureaucracy rarely moved with such speed. Everyone was shocked. A dedicated and valiant servant, Dr. Rizzo refused to kowtow to the powers that be and paid dearly for it.

There was a longstanding dispute between the Ombudsman's Office and the DBPR – "The Division" – regarding final authority over the Office of the Condominium Ombudsman. In the case of Dr. Rizzo's termination, the Legislature remained eerily silent. The Ombudsman was set up for failure. Powerful players did not want him to succeed. Yet he fooled his adversaries by surrounding himself with dedicated volunteers who helped him institute pervasive condo association election reform despite all obstacles.

Virgil was on the job for 18 months, and I was by his side for fifteen of those months. In that short duration, a handful of volunteer provided election monitor service to over 1.6 percent of Florida's 1.2 million condo unit owners. We moved at lightning speed - from 0 to 100 to a Full Stop with his termination. It is time for me to break my silence. Let the fireworks begin.

Chapter One
The Volunteer Staff

I served as Volunteer Chief Election Monitor for Florida's first Condominium Ombudsman from February 14, 2005 to May 1, 2006. During that time, I managed one of the four primary areas of responsibility under the Office of the Condominium Ombudsman. I served in 90 Petitioned Elections, was the lead monitor for 60 percent of those elections and processed 105 Election Monitor Petitions for validation by the Ombudsman. To my knowledge, I am still the only licensed Condominium Election Monitor in Florida.

How did all this come about? First and foremost, I was willing to devote time as a volunteer public servant. In July 2004, I submitted an application for appointment to the new Florida Advisory Council On Condominiums (ACC). On September 20, 2004, I received a letter from Florida Senator Jim King informing me that Peter Dunbar received the appointment for 2005. Dunbar also served as the chairperson for the Council in 2006.

When I heard that Peter Dunbar, "Mr. Condo Law Himself," was appointed, I felt relieved that I lost to such a highly well qualified individual. Mark Benson (who later became 2005 co-chair for the Council) was the second appointee. Senate appointments to the Council were now filled.

Condo Board Election Revolt!

On Valentine's Day 2005, I received a call from the Florida's first Condominium Ombudsman, Dr. Virgil Rizzo, who was appointed in December 2004. He asked if I would be interested in serving as a Volunteer Condominium Election Monitor. After discussing my background and the nature of the assignment, which was strictly to monitor elections, I agreed to give it a try. Little did I suspect how much that job would eventually entail.

Several days following Dr. Rizzo's initial call, he invited me to attend an election with him that very evening. "My baptism of fire," as he put it. Naturally, I agreed. It would be the first of workweeks without beginning or end for the next year and a half of my life. I was about to embark on a remarkable roller coaster ride. Virgil and I hit it off immediately. We're close in age. Moreover, we look so much alike that I was often mistaken for Virgil. We shared complementary personalities, a passion for the assignment and similar goals.

Nor did we stand on formality. We both called a spade a shovel. Aware of the problems such directness could cause, we felt that cutting to the chase also saved time when time was at a premium. Our word was our bond. If either of us committed to a task, it was carried out forthwith. Lord knows that we had little time to rehash old issues with so many new ones cropping up daily.

Condo Board Election Revolt!

We had a standing joke – that I was "The Hat." Whenever late, Virgil claimed that he was in the parking lot all along, waiting to see if I would come flying out of the building, thus saving him embarrassment. It was like throwing one's hat in the ring to see what would transpire. Indeed, while I operated on Vince Lombardi Time – "If you're not 15 minutes early, you're late" – Virgil was often late due to last minute emergencies.

He demonstrated confidence and trust by delegating so much responsibility. I was flattered until I realized that the Office of the Ombudsman would not be granted permanent staff for a long time to come. And once the word trickled out that a volunteer Election Monitor was in place, calls came pouring in at all times of the day, seven days a week.

Election reform also became a way of life for my wife, Doris – known to Virgil as "Betty". Little did we anticipate that she too would be conscripted; indeed, that Doris would become an integral part of my home-based operation. Taking fifty or more calls a week, she became extremely adept at recognizing callers by their voices and providing a personal touch. Most expected a recorded message. Discovering a real person at the other end of the line, there were many repeat callers. Many commented that it was refreshing to hear a cheerful, friendly voice.

Condo Board Election Revolt!

Unit owners, board members, property managers and even attorneys appreciated her warmth. At the Advisory Council on Condominiums (ACC) meeting held in Miami, in June 2005, Virgil told the assembly that while his two full-time employees at the Ft. Lauderdale office were extensions of his right arm, Doris and I were extensions of his left arm. That summed it up in a few words.

Virgil is not the typical lawyer. He uses fewer words than I'm using here to say the same thing. That taciturn quality led many to view him as curt and impolite. He had little time for social intercourse. When you're up to your waist in alligators, you don't spend time draining the swamp – and there was certainly an abundance of alligators. We started without procedures, guidelines, staff, office space, or funding, (dipping into our own pockets to get the operation up and running). Our primary resources included a complementary knowledge of condo statutes and the rules.

I spent the prior five years – from 2000 to 2005 – studying Florida community association statutes, while Dr. Rizzo was well-known for expertise in this arena. Our combined knowledge helped us develop a finely tuned election monitor system. I call it a "system" because it included all the elements required to develop an operation from scratch – and most specifically, to undertake the immense challenge of managing Petitioned Condominium Elections.

Condo Board Election Revolt!

We set energetic goals for ourselves from the outset. There was something new to be accomplished everywhere we turned. To meet these goals, it was vital to accommodate Virgil's schedule. Sixty to seventy-hour work weeks soon became the norm. Virgil had a habit of working very late at night. It was not uncommon for him to call at ten or eleven in the evening. To get even, I made it a practice to call him at nine in the morning to review the previous day's accomplishments or to provide him with an oral report on the prior evening's election.

During our discussions, we identified many flaws in condo statutes and rules that sorely required change. Every once in a while, Virgil – in the nicest way – would also make it clear that he needed me. I informed Virgil one Saturday morning that I was finally going to repair roof tile badly damaged by a prior hurricane. Virgil said, "I need you. Don't fall off or I'll kill you." I replied, "If I fall off, you won't have to." Moments like these made it all the more difficult to "retire" from my volunteer role in 2006, when I was finally replaced by a full time staff member.

In mid-April Virgil hired a new employee. Lucky for me the individual was one of our volunteer monitors. It made the transition easier. In parallel with that effort, we were successful in obtaining the services of a professional election company oriented in our procedures and ready to conduct elections on request.

Condo Board Election Revolt!

The transition was a fait accompli by the end of April and I was able to retire on May 1, 2006. My roller-coaster ride was over.

The work arrangement was simple: Virgil was the boss and I was the volunteer. It was that way from beginning to end. A large measure of what we accomplished must be credited to his leadership. Fortunately for both of us, I was willing and able to devote the time necessary to accomplish our shared objectives. Virgil knew that I was a self-starter with a "can do" attitude. A person can be his own greatest taskmaster. I proved that to Virgil time and time again, reinforcing his trust and confidence in my knowledge and abilities.

The duties required multi-tasking. Boy, did he multi-task. It also required flexibility. Virgil was always full of ideas and hot new priorities. It was often necessary to turn on a dime – a feat that tested me to the limit. In this brief period of time, Florida Condominium Unit Owners were provided with a high level of public service that they continue to expect.

Chapter Two
Genesis

There is an important history behind the creation of the Office of the Condominium Ombudsman. Long before this office was established, there was and still is an agency that condominium unit owners contact for resolution of association related problems. It is called the Division of Land Sales, Condominiums and Mobile Homes, a Division under the Department of Business and Professional Regulation (DBPR).

The Division regulates approximately 1.2 million condominium units that are governed by about 18,000 condominium associations. Florida taxpayers do not fund the Division. The Division is funded through an annual four dollar assessment paid by each unit owner. Unit owners reported that their complaints took too long to get resolved and often were left unresolved. These repeated complaints led to investigative steps by the legislature. In 2003, House Speaker Johnnie Byrd appointed a Select Committee on Condominiums Governance chaired by Miami/Dade's Honorable Representative Julio Robaina. Representative Robaina held Town Hall Meetings across the state, listening to complaints from owners.

After hearing thousands of complaints, Representative Robaina and the legislature recognized that there was a

Condo Board Election Revolt!

compelling lack of enforcement and accountability in current condo laws and that something had to be done about it.   Florida has the largest number of condominiums and homeowners' associations in the nation – with a projection that nearly 40 percent of all Florida residents will be living in a condo or in a house with an association governing them by 2010.

If the legislature failed to address the problem, it would only get worse. Armed with those facts, the legislature drafted new legislation in the 2004 legislative session. By the end of that session, the House and the Senate bills were identical, and Governor Jeb Bush signed the legislation into law.

The legislation created two new entities: the Office of the Condominium Ombudsman and the Advisory Council on Condominiums (ACC).   These entities would have overlapping responsibilities with the DBPR and with one another. Overlapping responsibilities and disagreement over the chain of command created a new turf war. By April 2005, it was rumored that efforts were under way to remove the Ombudsman from office. Much time would be spent by the ACC and by the Division trying to redefine, control, and regulate the activities of the Ombudsman. With these issues left unresolved, the events of June 1, 2006 were predictable. In April 2005, the Office of Program Policy & Analysis & Government Accountability (OPPAGA) issued a report on the DBPR (No. 05-24) that said:

Condo Board Election Revolt!

"Consumers file a wide range of complaints against condominiums. The Division Of Land Sales, Condominium and Mobile Homes does not close a significant number of consumer complaint cases and dispute arbitrations within intended time frames. The Division also typically responds to violations it finds [by] sending informational and warning letters rather than taking strong enforcement action such as levying fines. The Division and the Legislature could take several actions to improve the timeliness and effectiveness of the Division's services."

The OPPAGA report indicated that the legislature had taken important steps in trying to correct the problem by appointing Dr. Rizzo as Ombudsman and also guaranteed that his new office would receive an immense number of calls.

Condo Board Election Revolt!

Chapter Three
Operating Parameters

Section 5011 of Florida Statutes 718 (The Condominium Act) created the Office of the Ombudsman (Office) – which was located for administrative purposes within the Division of Florida Land Sales, Condominiums and Mobile Homes (Division). The Division is a subsection of the Department of Business and Professional Regulations (DBPR) and falls within the Legislative branch of the State Government. The Office of the Ombudsman is therefore a Bureau within the legislative branch attached to the Division, but outside the DBPR. I just said a mouthful, but it should become clearer shortly. Section 5011 required the Ombudsman to be appointed by and to serve at the will of the Governor. The appointee was required to be an attorney admitted to practice before the Florida Supreme Court. Dr. Rizzo was overqualified because he is both an attorney and a medical doctor.

The appointment made Dr. Rizzo a bureau chief of the Division, with staff and funds as is the case of all Division bureau chiefs. However, Dr. Rizzo's position was that of an administrative officer with specific authority granted by the Legislature. The Legislature, in effect, created a new Special Agency within the **Executive Branch** of the State Government, but outside of the control, direction and supervision of the DBPR.

Condo Board Election Revolt!

The Legislature created independent duties, powers and authority for the Ombudsman that were not within the control or direction of the Secretary of the DBPR. The legislative intent was to keep the Office separate from the Department – so that it could operate independently, without undue influence by the DBPR. The Ombudsman could properly and independently report on any subject matter, procedures, rules, personnel, and functions of the Division.

A 1974 Attorney General Opinion (AGO74-133) dealing with Governmental Reorganization clearly defined the authority of the DBPR Secretary as it related to other agencies. The powers of Department Heads or Secretaries were addressed in that opinion when it stated that a department head would be precluded from exercising authority over other departments.

The establishment of the Office of the Condominium Ombudsman falls under the category of Governmental Reorganization. Therefore, in my view, the opinion is applicable. Please don't be upset if you're still confused, because many of the players are as well. The Division and the Office of the Ombudsman were separate and independent, each having a different chain of command and different statutory mandates.

Condo Board Election Revolt!

The Division is indirectly under control of the Governor through the Secretary of the DBPR, whereas The Ombudsman is under the direct supervision of the Governor.

The Division has the power to enforce and ensure compliance with the provisions of the Condominium Act. The Office of the Ombudsman is mandated by statute to scrutinize, report, and make recommendations to the executive and legislative branches in reference to the problems identified within the Division and to make recommendations for change.

As advisor to the Governor and to the Legislature regarding necessary changes to improve the function and procedures of Division, the Ombudsman could not effectively perform those duties without creating internal conflict and controversy with the DBPR! In my opinion, the office of the Ombudsman should have been attached to the Attorney General's office and provided limited subpoena power.

If there is a State organization chart showing the Ombudsman's reporting relationships, I have not come across it in my research. Keep in mind that the Ombudsman, by statute, was required to do thefollowing as stated in FS 718.5012(3): "To prepare and issue reports and recommendations to the Governor, the department, the division, the Advisory Council on Condominiums, the President of the Senate, and the Speaker of the House of Representatives on any matter or subject within the jurisdiction of the division. The ombudsman shall make recommendations he or she deems appropriate for legislation relative to division procedures, rules, jurisdiction, personnel, and functions."

This wording is right out of the statute. It is what the Legislature instructed him to do. How effective could he be when reporting to the very organization that he was required to report on? I keep reinforcing this relationship because I'm trying to connect all the dots for you. These are important points to remember as you read the rest of my story.

Financing for the Office comes from the Condo Trust Fund, which also finances the Division. (Each unit owner pays four dollars annually to the Condo Trust Fund.) As such, the Office is funded by condo owners and not by the taxpayers of the State.

When I asked Dr. Rizzo about events surrounding his appointment in December 2004, he told me there was little fanfare. He simply received a call from a member of the Governor's staff informing him of his appointment as the Condominium Ombudsman by the Governor. Virgil asked the caller what he was supposed to do next. He was assured that someone would get back to him.

Condo Board Election Revolt!

When he did not hear back from the Governor's office, Virgil decided to travel to Tallahassee. Upon arrival, he asked to see Governor Jeb Bush, but was told that the Governor refused to meet with him. Remaining in the capitol for several days, he subsequently encountered the Governor shaking hands with people on the sidewalk during the lunch hour. Virgil extended his hand to the Governor and introduced himself. When Virgil explained that he was the new Ombudsman, Governor Jeb Bush said, "Yes, you are famous." The Governor then walked away. Later that week Virgil received his official letter of appointment.

Virgil's new duties were spelled out in Section 5012 of the Florida Statutes, the Ombudsman's powers and duties section. That section stated that he had the powers necessary to carry out the duties of his Office as listed in nine subsections, which can be combined into four categories. I equate these four categories with a four-legged stool, namely: Division Change Recommendations; Education; Conflict Resolution; and Election Monitoring. The meaning of "he had the powers necessary to carry out the duties of his office" would be constantly challenged.

As a volunteer election monitor, my primary focus and interest was obviously on the last leg of that stool – Election Monitoring – because that section defined my operating parameters, specifically Paragraph 9 of FS 718.5012 which reads: "Fifteen percent of the total

Condo Board Election Revolt!

voting interests in a condominium association, or six unit owners, whichever is greater, may petition the ombudsman to appoint an election monitor to attend the annual meeting of the unit owners and conduct the election of directors. The ombudsman shall appoint a Division employee, a person or persons specializing in condominium election monitoring, or an attorney licensed to practice in this state as the election monitor. All costs associated with the election monitoring process shall be paid by the association. The Division shall adopt a rule establishing procedures for the appointment of election monitors and the scope and extent of the monitor's role in the election process."

In addition to this statute, there were other guidelines for the creation of operating parameters: Florida's Regular Election Statute (FS 718.112(2)(d)(3)); the associated section of the Florida Administrative Code (FAC), Chapter 61B-23.0021; and The Ombudsman: Election Monitor Role: Scope and Extent (FS Chapter 61B-23.00215). These statutes and rules grant the Division of Land Sales, Condominiums and Mobile Homes the authority to put in force administrative rules – once it is determined that the proposed rule is necessary in order to implement, enforce or interpret provisions of the statute.

However, any proposed rule cannot conflict with the statute itself. The rule as it applied to election monitoring was established and, therefore, it had to be followed. For now we will only concern ourselves with the section of the FAC rule that deals with the Election Monitor Role (FS 61B-23.00215) and describes the Petitioned Election Monitor Process. These rules were our operating parameters.

The FAC provides a good description on voting instructions, but the law does not require the association to provide it to their members! I frequently recommended that associations should be required by law to provide voting instructions to their members. Keep in mind: At the time, there was no organization in place to execute these parameters. All we had was a one-man band, namely Dr. Rizzo. We functioned with the understanding that Dr. Rizzo had the full powers necessary to carry out the duties vested in him by the 2004 Florida Legislature. There were immediate challenges that had to be addressed. We made adjustments accordingly. Virgil called it "a work in progress." It was indeed.

Challenge #1: The law was now in effect. If a petition was received that met the criteria, it had to be honored. Monitors must be assigned and the election conducted on the date, time and place as requested.

Challenge #2: The DBPR did not have or require a standard methodology for conducting elections. It was not in that "business." Until Dr. Rizzo's appointment, DBPR officials functioned as "observers" at disputed elections. Therefore, the DBPR found it unnecessary to create its own set of election monitoring mechanics. Election monitors came from three sources: Division employees; a person or persons specialized in condominium elections; or an attorney licensed to practice in the state. By contrast, there were no state election monitors. Virgil was our attorney, and thanks to my previous knowledge and Virgil's tutoring, I quickly became the person specialized in condominium election monitoring.

Challenge #3: Then there was the issue of payment for the monitors, which I will discuss later. As Chief Election Monitor, I was able to identify many shortcomings in the condo regular election statutes and rules. I provided my input to the Ombudsman, which he included with his recommendations to the legislature. Ultimately, we received the same disappointing results with our statute change recommendations that we did with our FAC recommendations. For most of the 2006 legislative session, it appeared that legislators had thrown up their hands and returned home.

I've left the legislative topic for last in the hope that the last thing read will be the thing most remembered. If the legislature were to pick up the ball and run on these suggested changes, Florida condo owners would be well served. I hope the reader is getting a clear picture of the myriad challenges that confronted us. We had more questions than answers. We were in the full throes of planning, trying to answer Who? What? When? Where? Why? and How? Election monitoring requests were pouring in.

As we had no funds to hire new troops, it was clear that we needed volunteers as soon as possible. Virgil also knew that it would not be easy to find qualified candidates once funds were available because the pay level would be modest. It was therefore essential to bring volunteers up to speed as fast as possible – before demand overran capability. Ask yourself what would you have done in his position? The statutory requirement was in place, but there was no funding, no organization, no procedures and no staff. Would you tell the requester to call back next year? Or would you improvise as Dr. Rizzo did to meet the demand as we began developing the Volunteer Election Monitor Organization.

Dr. Rizzo received criticism for the way he was forced to operate in the beginning. The ACC and the Division, a full-blown bureaucracy, was constantly accusing him of being out of control. He was bringing organization and stability to an outstanding idea, but an idea that was ill implemented and chaotic. The bureaucracy was not ready for this new statute. To improve responsiveness and overcome the manpower shortage, we had to organize rapidly. This became our foremost priority.

Condo Board Election Revolt!

Chapter Four
Creating the Organization

Creating a responsive organization was a daunting task. A totally new system was required. Indeed, we took the same approach that a software programmer applies when developing a major software system: attacking the challenge one module at a time. We soon determined that following practices and procedures were essential:

- Petition validation
- Billing methodology
- Noticing standard
- Monitor staffing and qualification
- Communication apparatus
- Reporting standards
- Election mechanics
- Filing system
- Statistic data collection
- Unit owner election training
- Statute and Rule change input methodology

Dr. Rizzo operated from his condo with a laptop and his cell phone. I relied on my home computer and telephone. We took the IBM "Completed Staff Work" approach which I taught it many times in IBM management classes. For those unfamiliar with the term, Completed Staff Work is a simple but demanding

Condo Board Election Revolt!

concept. Basically, it means to perform a task to the point where only your direct supervisor signs off on the work because it is that complete. Easy enough. While some would use the word "professional" to describe this process, relatively few comprehend what that word entails.

Completed Staff Work is even more specific in that it clearly defines expectations in performance in measurable terms. Requiring a high degree of delegation from your supervisor, it's an excellent model to employ when you don't have time to do it all yourself, as was Dr. Rizzo's case. This does not mean that the boss abdicates his responsibilities. He can delegate with abandon, but is always shouldered with accountability. One must use this model wisely. Virgil and I understood that. At no time did I take unilateral actions.

Everything was reviewed prior to implementation within the context of completed staff work. We were in agreement that my part of the effort would be run like a business, but that I was not going into business. I was a volunteer and wished to remain one. In addition, I did not care for the limelight, which stole precious time from performing the tasks at hand. The public relations part of the job was his – where it rightly belonged. I was the silent partner, filling in the void as needed. For that reason, few were aware of my role unless we had a direct encounter.

Condo Board Election Revolt!

Case in Point: On March 11, 2006, the Wall Street Journal featured a front-page article about the Office of the Condominium Ombudsman. The reporter had previously contacted Dr. Rizzo, stating that he wanted to produce a feature article on our volunteer election monitoring program. Virgil, in turn, asked him to contact me. I spent several hours talking with the reporter. After our first conversation, I received a call from Virgil saying, "What did you tell this guy? He's all fired up. Now he wants to fly down to attend one of your elections, and he's going to talk to his editor about doing several more articles. He's planning to call the people you identified as possible contacts."

Sure enough, the reporter called back to inquire when I would monitor the next election. Fortunately, we had two big elections coming up on the same night. I was the team leader for one and Virgil for the other. I convinced him to attend the election at which Virgil would officiate. I also put him in touch with the attorney representing the unit owners, so that she could invite him as her guest.

The reporter flew down in advance to conduct background interviews and meet with our staff. Unfortunately, Dr. Rizzo ended up in the hospital two days prior to the election and was not able to preside. However, the reporter was present and wrote his article. If you read that article, you won't find my name (as planned). Unfortunately, you also won't find the

Condo Board Election Revolt!

name of the volunteer election monitors assigned to and responsible for the election, those who worked all night and wrote the report the following day. The article featured two regular office employees whose main duties had nothing to do with volunteer election monitoring program, nor were they assigned to the election. Their duties relating to petitioned elections were to pass on messages to my office for follow-up. However, they managed to capture the spotlight intended for volunteer election monitors who conducted the election. While the report was a public relations coup for the office, we had also hoped to provide justly deserved recognition for our volunteers.

One day I received a call from Virgil informing me I had a recorded message at the office. He insisted that I come to the office as soon as possible to hear it myself. The message was from a senator in Washington D.C., stating that I had been selected as businessman of the year for my region. A call-back number was also included. I said, "This is a joke, right?" Virgil dialed the number. A man answered and identified himself as the senator's staff assistant. Virgil introduced himself as the Florida Condominium Ombudsman and handed the phone to me. The senator's staff assistant congratulated me and invited me to Washington to attend a black-tie award banquet. I told him that I was honored, but would not be able to attend. When I hung up the phone, Virgil looked at me with disbelief and asked, "Why did you do that?" "You're the PR guy, not me," I replied.

Condo Board Election Revolt!

"But they're giving you the award," he answered. "They gave it to the wrong guy. I don't have time for that and I don't have a tux," I said. "You can rent a tux," Virgil responded. "I'm paying for enough stuff now," I replied. We both laughed and that was the end of it.

Condo Board Election Revolt!

Chapter Five
Election Parameters

It is important to describe the normal condominium election process. The question may come to mind: "How can such a simple, straightforward process cause so much trouble?" As I see it, there are two reasons. The first is that the majority of volunteer association directors don't have a clue as to what the statutes and rules require of them. That is why mandatory education should be provided.

I know you'll tell me that the association directors are only volunteers. My response is they have awesome power and responsibilities. The quality of life for everyone in an association depends on the competency of their directors. If directors are unwilling to take the time to learn the job, they shouldn't take it on. Knowledge of his/her position is a director's fiduciary responsibility. If one chooses not to be responsible, he/she does not belong in the job. An association may be better off in receivership than in the hands of an incompetent board. In receivership, the association pays for board services, but they are carried out in a legally prescribed manner. Regardless, owners pay a high price. Ineptitude is expensive; though sometimes the cost is not obvious.

Condo Board Election Revolt!

The second answer is obvious: The election process is knowingly manipulated and mangled by knowledgeable boards with agendas or by property managers and attorneys that don't want to lose cash-cow accounts. Board members who understand their responsibilities and conduct themselves as sincere volunteers have the right attitude. They recognize that their role is to **serve** as a board member – with an emphasis on serve. You seldom hear from these associations.

Effective education would reduce election complaints by as much as 50 percent. Enforcement might take care of another forty percent of the complaints. You'll never eliminate them entirely. As the old saying goes, "There is no behavior change without consequence." I'll have more to say about this later when I discuss Division enforcement. Let's move on to the overview and the complexity of the regular election process.

Question #1: What is required to hold an election? Answer: First, association bylaws declare when the annual election must be held. If you have the same number of candidates as vacancies, you don't need an election. If a member of the board resigns before his/her term expires, you don't need an election. The remaining board members appoint someone to fill the vacancy for the remainder of the term. If there are more candidates than there are vacancies, you may have an election. I say "may," because 20 percent of the association's authorized voters must participate, otherwise you don't have an election. Then what, you ask? In that event, the "holdover doctrine" kicks in. The holdover doctrine makes it incumbent on the current board to continue to exercise the powers of the association until successor board members are appointed or elected.

The 20 percent requirement is an arbitrary and meaningless number that confers greater power on those who decide not to vote than on those who actually vote if apathy is prevalent. In my opinion, this is a violation of civil and contractual rights of those wishing to vote and those wishing to run for office. Both groups are having their rights denied. It also leaves individuals in office whose term of office has expired. If only one owner voted and no one was denied the right to vote, that voter should determine the outcome of the election. There are no voter number or percentage limits in municipal elections. My message to the apathetic voters is this: "Elections Matter." Elections are the single most influential event in condo living. It affects your quality of life. Don't surrender to apathy. Not too complicated so far? Then let's raise the next question.

Question #2: Who can or can't vote? Answer: Obviously, unit owners can. Again, those bylaws must be referenced. The association may require voter certificates for multiple unit owners. That is where all the owners of a unit decide which one of them will be the designated, authorized voter. They all sign the certificate and it stays in force until a new one is filed with the association. Corporations and trusts have to do the same if they wish to vote. By the way, only the individual named on the voter certificate can assign someone else proxy power to vote for other non-election association business. So who can't vote? No unit owner shall permit any other person to vote his or her ballot. Renters, individuals with power of attorney and proxy holders cannot vote in a regular election.

In my humble view, holders of Powers Of Attorney should be permitted to vote in regular condominium elections. This restriction is inconsistent with recall procedures, where a holder of POA can participate in the recall process. For example, granted a power of attorney, one can buy, or sell a condo for another party and can even authorize a doctor to remove that individual from life support – but it is no assurance that you will be able to cast a vote on behalf of that person in a condo election. As it is, many associations disregard this rule. Why not fix the law?

Question #3: How many ways can I vote? Answer: You do not have to personally deliver your ballot to the association. Otherwise, how could you give it to the mailman to deliver? There are several ways to vote. Obviously, you can mail your ballot. You can drop it off at the office. You can give it to a neighbor to bring it to the election for you. Or you can bring it to the election meeting yourself. And if for some reason, you did not receive a ballot or lost the one you did receive, you can request another ballot and relevant envelopes at the meeting. The association is required to have some on hand and to allow you to vote in person. If you're out of town and did not receive a voting package, you can prepare your own ballot with the candidates' names. Use your own two envelopes, making certain that the outside clearly shows your printed name, unit number and signature. These three items are key in ensuring that your outer envelope is validated and that your vote will be counted. Mail it directly to the association or to a friend who can bring it to the election for you.

Question #4: Who can run for the board? Answer: As far as the State of Florida goes, there is only one restriction. You can't be a board member if you are a felon who has not had his/her rights to vote restored. That's it. For association-related restrictions, again we have to check the bylaws. Some will require you be a unit owner, others will require permanent residence, etc. So this question may require follow-up if you intend to run for the board but don't know if you qualify. That leads us to the next question.

Question #5: How does the election come about? Answer: The process is launched through notification and delivery procedures. First, I'll give you an easy way to remember election milestone dates. Remember this number sequence: 60-40-35-34 to 14 and you have all the relevant dates of a regular election schedule. They include the dates of all events that must take place before election day. Now let's take them one at a time to see what events take place at each of these scheduled milestones.

60 Days Before The Election: The FIRST notice of election is sent to the unit owners. It announces the date, time, and place of the election. A properly prepared notice provides the candidacy cut-off date, the candidate information sheet submission cut-off date, and instructions for completion of the information sheet. Included are the agenda of the meeting and the correct address to which to mail your candidacy.

40 Days Before The Election: This date is the cut-off date for submitting your candidacy. If you wish to be on the ballot, you have to make sure the association or the designated election agent receives it before the cut-off date. So how do you do that? You do it by personal delivery or by Certified Mail Return Receipt Requested. The association is required to provide a written receipt, but if it doesn't, you still have proof of timely submission.

35 Days Before The Election: That is the cut-off date for submitting your information sheet to be included with the ballot. Send it in with your candidacy to make certain that it arrives on time and that you have proof that it did so without incurring additional mailing costs.

Condo Board Election Revolt!

The rules on the information sheet itself are straightforward. You are allowed a one-sided 8.5"x11" sheet of paper.

If you wish to write your message in two languages, it will cut your space in half. What you say is up to you. The association cannot change any of it, even if you misspell your name. Also, if it's handwritten and nobody can read your handwriting, that's the way it's going to be printed. If you and other candidates don't use a full page, the association may ask your permission to combine yours with someone else's, but it can't combine if you don't agree. However, for economy's sake, the association can print different information sheets on two-sided paper. In fairness, however, the information sheet should appear in the same order as the names on the ballot, alphabetically by surname. Now the association has all it needs to prepare the election package.

34 To 14 Days Before The Election: The SECOND notice is sent to the unit owners. It can be sent out anywhere from 34 to 14 days prior to the election. Typically, the association has everything ready to go and can ship early; sometimes they get information sheets on the last day and have clerical work that places a delay in sending out the materials. For associations that have many non-permanent resident owners, it is wise to send the notice out early. I can't count how many times out-of-town unit owners had to overnight mail their

Condo Board Election Revolt!

ballots to me or called to complain because they still had not received their ballots.

The second notice should not contain any editorial comments for or against the candidates nor should it include any endorsements. The package should contain the ballot, an outer envelope addressed to the person or entity authorized to vote with name, unit number and a space for your signature. Also included should be a smaller inner envelope for the ballot, candidate information sheets, the meeting agenda and optionally, voting instructions in two languages where appropriate.

The association is not required to provide voting instructions even though they are well defined in the FAC. To avoid voter confusion, associations should be creative in the way they handle other voter record and annual business meeting issues – for example, voter certificates, proxies, proxy envelopes and business meeting voting matters. The association is not required to provide an affidavit of mailing for the second notice, as it has to do for the first notice. Does that make sense to you? The association must provide proof that it notified you of an election, but it doesn't have to provide proof that it sent you a ballot to vote!

Question 6: What about the actual election? Answer: Well, the next thing that is required to hold the election is an impartial election committee. The rules on who can serve on that committee are simple. You have to be

Condo Board Election Revolt!

a unit owner. You can't be a current board member, an officer, a candidate or a spouse of any of the above. Basically, the impartial committee has two responsibilities: to validate the outer envelopes and to count the ballots. Do these duties ring a bell? They should, because these requirements are identical to the duties of election monitors.

The impartial committee can perform pre-validation of ballots on hand on the same day of the election or before the election, as long as the pre-validation has been officially "noticed" and the membership can attend to observe.. Otherwise, that task is performed at the election. At the election, members should be allowed to vote up until the outer envelope validation process is completed, at which time the poll should be announced closed, just prior to opening the first outer envelope.

Both the outer envelope validation process and the vote counting take place in the presence of the unit owners in attendance. What if we end up with a tie for the last board vacancy? What do we do? If any of the individuals involved in the tie (and there may be more than two) are willing to withdraw from the election, thus leaving a single candidate, then the single remaining candidate involved in the tie fills the vacancy. Otherwise, a run-off election is required and the association has seven days to send out an election notice.

Condo Board Election Revolt!

Only the candidates involved in the tie can be on the ballot and their original information sheets are sent out once again. The run-off election cannot be held for at least twenty-one days and no more than thirty days after the original election. It's all handled the same as a new second-notice package. Finally, all election materials must be retained for one year. Unit owners can inspect them, on request.

There you have it, a simple description of the Florida condominium regular election process. So tell me, how can property managers, attorneys, and board of directors so mismanage this process? Either they don't know what they are doing or they know exactly what they are doing. Everything I addressed here is covered in Florida Statute Chapter 718.112(2)(d)(3) and Chapter 61B-23.0021 of the Florida Administrative Code. Every board member can be taught this process in two hours. We taught at every election we conducted by show-and-tell. We explained every step of the process, and we left trained unit owners behind – specifically, those that served as impartial committee members. They received On The Job Training (OJT), if you will. There is no excuse for ignorance, unless associations intentionally break the rules or, worse yet, commit election fraud. We helped Dr. Rizzo meet his legislative mandate by educating unit owners. We did so face-to-face in a practical manner.

Chapter Six
Petition Processing

Petition processing put the gears in motion that activated the most effective and controversial part of the new 2004 condo statute. For a detailed description of the process, refer to Appendix C and Appendix D. This section of the statute provides people power. If 15 percent of an association requested intervention, intervention they received. For the first time, someone other than the association board of directors had the authority to conduct a board of director election.

Never before did a party have authority to tell the board, the property manager, or even the attorney that they were now spectators instead of players. Trust me when I say that this message did not go over well. In time, it would not go unpunished. The program was too successful for its own good. Incumbent board members lost their bid for reelection 50 percent of the time, which meant that property managers and attorneys were losing clients.

The cost of keeping old boards in power was being revealed. As word spread, more associations signed up for the service. The opposition cried about our lack of neutrality. Much has been made about the new Ombudsman's promise of neutrality. To that I say, "Good Luck." In my experience, neutrality is a luxury

Condo Board Election Revolt!

in condominium elections. Either the board or the petitioner was right. You had to move in the direction that the facts warranted. We made friends and enemies of board of directors, property managers, attorneys, and unit owners – all at the same time. When boards, property managers and attorneys cooperated, there were few complaints about our role. We received cooperation from some and resistance from others.

A few associations never wanted to hear from us again, while others asked that we conduct the following year's election. That is the nature of the Ombudsman's job. There is no neutrality when it comes to resolving conflict. The statute and the facts dictate the position to be taken by the Ombudsman. Fair assessment and fair treatment based on the facts are all that the condominium community can expect from the Office of the Condominium Ombudsman. It was our starting point every time a new election monitor petition request arrived. Once the original petition was received, two copies were made, one for my use and one to be sent to the board of directors of the association.

First, I checked the association against the corporation filing records, in order to confirm the association's address, the name of its agent, the size of its board of directors and names of directors. I accessed the Property Appraiser's (PA) record for the most recent list of unit owners, in order to verify the number of units in the association and to correctly determine the required

Condo Board Election Revolt!

15 percent participation for validation. The Property Appraiser list was then downloaded into a database for unit number and alpha sorting and printing. Some associations used alpha rosters while others used unit number rosters – thus both were required. Using the printed list, the petition was checked for unit ownership. Follow-ups were made if and when the ownership was in question, unless more than the required 15 percent had already been validated. Results of the check were provided to the Ombudsman, who made the actual validation and drafted the notice to be sent to the association.

Validating a petition took me as little as four hours for smaller associations and several days for larger ones. I expended over two hundred hours during a five-month period on one particular association. Often, we had the minimum amount of time to prepare for an election, but occasionally we had a long lead time. I spent considerable time traveling back and forth from my home to the office at 1400 West Commercial Boulevard in Fort Lauderdale and to the post office. MapQuest was used to obtain the directions, distance and travel time to associations. These directions were confirmed with petitioners and sometimes better directions were obtained as a result.

The location and size of the association determined the number of required monitors and which ones should best attend. Individual availability was always a concern. Election time estimates were based on a projected 60 percent participation. Armed with all those factors, it was possible to prepare the invoice. That invoice, along with the election notice and a copy of the petition, was sent to the association. Cost of service was always provided. The average charge for a petitioned condo election was approximately $300 per election. Because some associations had lied to their membership, telling them that it would cost thousands for our services, we made procedural adjustments to correct that problem – and they worked quite well.

I remember two specific claims. One association erroneously reported a cost of $5000 when the true cost was 10 percent of that amount. Another association erroneously reported a cost of $7000 when the true cost was less than 10 percent of that amount. In both instances, their membership was told that fee was high because the monitors were traveling from Tallahassee – with all associated expenses – when in fact all monitors were local.

That ploy was used to turn the rest of the association against the petitioners. To stop the dissemination of false information and to reduce pressure on petitioners, we changed the notice of election and the invoice, instructing the association to post both upon receipt on the association's official bulletin board. As usual, some associations complied immediately upon receipt; others only did so when we followed up after being informed

Condo Board Election Revolt!

that they had not complied. Many associations refused to announce that we were coming, fearing that our presence might generate a heavier turnout – which was typically the case.

Our notice-posting request resulted in a new awareness on the part of the membership. They were now privy to the fee structure for our services, which in turn, often led to questions by association members regarding what the condo attorney was charging for his services...and for what purpose.

I remember a direct confrontation between a unit owner and the attorney, who to my surprise told the owner that he was receiving his regular fee of $325/hour portal to portal. The unit owner's subsequent question was, "What are we getting for that tonight? It appears that the Election Monitors are doing all the work and you're doing the watching. Or better yet, are we paying you four to five times what we're paying him so he can teach you how an election is supposed to be conducted?" (We were not very popular with some condo attorneys.)

Approximately 10 percent of the associations that used our services also chose to have at least two attorneys present. Why two? Your guess is as good as mine. As to the cost, you can easily do the math. Receiving a copy of the petition, several boards relied upon an interesting ploy, otherwise known as harassment. There was typically an acceleration in phone calls to our office once the petition was mailed to the association. I can't count how many times I received petitioner complaints once the board had the petition in hand. The most frequent complaint: a petitioner was told by board members that he/she would be required to pay the cost of our services.

My response: "That's true, but did he also tell you that everybody else in your association will also pay? It's a service provided to all members of the association." They typically replied, "He didn't tell me that." Others would call telling me they were being grilled as to why they would do such a thing. Some were pressured to sign a new petition to reverse the first one! There was the elder citizen who told her board that if they didn't stop knocking on her door, she was going to file a complaint with the police. The petition reversal campaign at that condo came to a dead stop. I recall receiving a complaint about a signature on one of the petitions that did not match the unit owner's signature. So I followed up. Yes, the lady was the owner. No, she herself had not signed the petition, but asked her caregiver to sign it on her behalf in front of two witnesses. The woman was blind, regularly conducted association business in this manner and her association was aware of that.

So why challenge this one? This petitioner had received precisely the percentage of signatures required. If they could eliminate one signature, the board would be the

Condo Board Election Revolt!

victor. I can count on one hand the times we were unable to approve a petition because of a late submission. After questioning a petitioner, Boards would sometimes claim that the petitioner "admitted" that he did not know what he or she was signing.

I received many questions and heard many comments from outraged callers. Put yourself in their position. Assume you had contacted the Division some time ago to resolve a problem, but you were still at point zero. Suddenly, instead of listening to a recorded voice, you were able to talk to a "real person" on a Saturday or Sunday or even at ten o'clock at night. How would you communicate all that stored frustration? Perhaps you would perform a memory dump on that patient ear at the other end of the phone. I made certain the caller was aware that I was not an attorney and was not dispensing advice. And how could I forget that we had no actual enforcement authority? I also always tried to keep the conversation on track with the election issue at hand. It was not always easy. When they began recounting the election irregularities, I eventually had to shatter their hope by informing them they had to contact the Division about the problem.

The typical response: "I've already contacted the Division and nothing happened. That's why I'm calling you." I had to tell them that I was only authorized to validate and count, that is to make sure the authorized person voted and that the votes were counted correctly.

Condo Board Election Revolt!

It was much easier to convey this message over the phone than it was to do so in person at the election. Looking the petitioner in the eyes when I shared this information, I could readily observe a look of disappointment and occasionally hear, "What am I paying you for if you can't do anything about this? This is why I ask for your help."

I recall one election where a petitioner was waiting for me in the lobby with a ballot in hand. He said that he was a candidate, but his name was not on the ballot. He showed me a copy of the first notice and his return receipt as proof that he submitted his candidacy letter in time and that it was received before the cut-off date. His name should have been on the ballot. I told him that he had a legitimate complaint and should file it with the Division.

There was absolutely nothing I could do about putting his name on the ballot or canceling the election for that matter. I did not have that authority. All I could do was point out the error to the board. His reply was, "Don't bother, they already know."

Questions raised were typically about election rules and mechanics. I could easily answer those inquiries because I was quoting directly from the statute and/or the rule. There were many reasons for petition requests and many stated the same reasons. Here is a list of

Condo Board Election Revolt!

reasons that condo owners gave for requesting our services. It's not in any particular order, nor is it complete. Some listed several reasons in one petition:

1. Did not receive ballot;
2. Name left off the ballot;
3. Illegal candidate on the ballot;
4. Could not vote at the election. No ballots available;
5. Voting cut off before the election meeting;
6. Wrong election date, place, or time on election notice;
7. Change of election site at last minute without notice;
8. Doors locked at start of meeting;
9. Not allowed to observe pre-election validation;
10. Votes counted in privacy;
11. Votes counted by the board or manager.
12. Pre-validation without notice;
13. Ballots removed from outer envelopes before the election, outer envelopes shredded;
14. All second-notice materials not included;
15. Ballots mailed too late to return;
16. Ballots not sent to out-of-town owners;
17. Ballots found after the election were counted and results changed;
18. Not publicizing the candidate cut-off date;
19. Names on the ballot are out of order, incumbents are listed first;
20. Short incumbent bio on the ballot;
21. Allowed proxy voting;
22. Allowed power of attorney voting;
23. Deceased unit owner voting;
24. Allowed renter to vote;
25. Previous owner voting for new owner who is away;

Condo Board Election Revolt!

26. Lost voter certificate;
27. Voter certificate book not updated;
28. Allow corporations to vote without voter certificates;
29. Ballots sent to incumbent candidate president's home;
30. Second notice sent without a ballot;
31. Second notice sent without voting envelopes;
32. Instructed to put ballot in the proxy envelope;
33. Instructed to put the voter certificate in with the ballot;
34. No qualified voter list;
35. Using sign-in sheet as qualified voter list;
36. Using mailing address as roster;
37. Ballot turned in by anyone but owner is disregarded;
38. Ballots with fewer than the allowed voting number are disregarded;
39. Property manager counts the votes without witnesses;
40. None of the directors are unit owners as required by the bylaws;
41. No election conducted as required by the bylaws;
42. Vote tally number greater than the number of units;
43. Legitimate ballots disregarded;
44. Told how to cast vote at the election;
45. Loss of anonymity class or fractional voting
46. Ballot tampering;
47. Refuse to accept copied ballots;
48. Disregarded because ballot written on;
49. Accepting unsigned outer envelopes;
50. Allowing other unit owners to vote for absent unit owners.

Condo Board Election Revolt!

I could go on, but fifty should provide insight into the flaws of the condo election process. It may be of interest to note that the original version of the condo bill in 2004 contained a provision granting the Ombudsman subpoena powers, but this provision was subsequently removed because the legislature felt such power was too dangerous – given the lack of oversight over the Ombudsman.

If the Ombudsman had been granted subpoena powers, many of the shenanigans he encountered would have been history. There were outbursts of anger, frustration and outrage at many of these elections. More than once, the police were present to ensure that the situation did not get out of hand. They usually left once the election began. I knew what I was going to face when I walked into the lion's den. No matter what the circumstances, we had to remain focused, fair and impartial. We were there to conduct an election. Period.

Approximately 80 percent of the petitioners requested that the ballots be sent to our office and that we bring these ballots to the election. Ballot tampering was the petitioners number one concern. We could forward the request, but associations were not required to honor it. On the other hand, numerous associations, property managers and attorneys welcomed the free service, recognizing its value. If the ballots were sent to the Ombudsman, associations, attorneys and property managers could not be accused of ballot tampering or

Condo Board Election Revolt!

destroying ballots, etc. Imagine that a simple change in the return address on a ballot envelope was sufficient to put such fears to rest.

There were instances where associations wanted to use the service, but the request came too late; second-notice materials were already prepared for mailing. On several occasions, the petition reached us at the tail end of the election cycle, yet petitioners unfairly accused their association of refusing to cooperate with us. I made it a point to politely remind those petitioners that better planning on their part would have yielded the result they wanted, because the association was willing to honor the request.

It's important to note here that petitioners were not always right. When an association was genuine in its cooperation, elections proceeded smoothly and often-time, the incumbents were re-elected.

As they say, "I report, you decide." Sometimes what appears to be cooperation leaves you wondering. Case in point: I monitored an election where the property manager, who for all intents and purposes ran the association, agreed to have the ballots sent to my post office box. I suggested that he obtain board approval for the decision, which he did. What he suggested, they accepted. The petitioner was also pleased with that decision. In the end, however, we received fewer than twenty ballots from this 150-member association. When

Condo Board Election Revolt!

the election was held, only a handful of owners voted in person, yet the 20 percent voting requirement was met. As I recall, the incumbent board swept the election by a four to one margin.

Condo Board Election Revolt!

Chapter Seven
Election Mechanics

Although a volunteer, I represented the Governor and the Legislature. We repeatedly reminded volunteer election monitors that their actions would affect the quality of life for all the unit owners until the next election. A fair and impartial election was expected. We had to deliver and get it right. Quality performance was expected by the board, the property manager, the attorney, and all unit owners – present or absent – as well as the Legislature.

We were also accused of bias on several occasions, because our monitors for those elections included members of Cyber Citizens For Justice, Inc. (CCFJ). Yet, none of our critics mentioned that several monitors were also members of CAI. In fact, the split was about equal in members belonging to CCFJ, CAI, and those having no affiliation with any organization. We had a mix at all of our elections. Moreover, in the last few months they were heavily represented by a CAI-affiliated monitor.

The point that I wish to make here: "It's how you do your job." While many of us belonged to various organizations, we also did our best to compartmentalize those affiliations from the task at hand. We often wondered: were those leveling charges affiliated with

Condo Board Election Revolt!

organizations? We constantly reminded our volunteers that the 2004 Florida Legislature mandated our role. The matter at hand sorely required attention. We also had a strict rule. During the election, petitioners would not receive preferential treatment. Everyone was entitled to equal attention. All eyes were on us. We resided in a goldfish bowl. For previous elections, records and completed files were typically sparse. As we improved the system, the files also became more complete.

I prepared a workbook for my use or for the attending monitor's use for every election. The workbook contained copies of the petition, the notice of election, our invoice, and the property appraiser's list sorted in both numerical and alphabetical order. Corporations and trusts were highlighted, as were the multiple unit owners on the alphabetical list in different colors, for quick identification.

If a first and or second notice was provided, it was also attached, as was a copy of the original ballot that had been obtained from the association – or from the petitioner when the association did not provide it in a timely manner. In addition, we had two sets of pre-prepared voter tally worksheet forms. One set was identified as the association's record of the election tally and the other as the Ombudsman's set of election records. Also available were team rollup summary worksheets and impartial committee sign-in sheets; again one set for the association and one for the

Condo Board Election Revolt!

Ombudsman's records. Armed with all those materials, we performed our job efficiently. All we required from the association was their authorized voter list and their voter certificate book, if they used one and if they enforced voter certificate use.

These complex preparations helped establish our credibility. They also came at a cost: time. Time was in precious supply before an election. We had a standard charge for this service – identified as a Petition Administration Cost on the invoice. The cost was $50 for associations of 100 or fewer units, $100 for associations from 100 to 300 units, and $150 for associations over 300 units. It did not cover costs for my supplies, let alone my time.

I spent, on average, between twelve and twenty hours preparing materials for the typical election, filing these materials and retrieving them whenever I received a piece necessary to complete the package. There were many phone call follow-ups and additional trips to the post office or the to the office at West Commercial Boulevard. I was also immersed in online research, downloads, the creation of databases, and the production of tally worksheets. Yet, the Petition Administration Cost covered only the cost of travel to the office, travel to the post office, and operating supplies. It was a great moneymaker.

Condo Board Election Revolt!

There are five points during the ballot handling process where a unit owner's ballot can be disregarded and not counted. Therefore, it is incumbent upon the election committee members to: understand the 'rules of disregard;' to ensure that only valid ballots are counted; to ensure that no valid ballot is disregarded; and to avoid disenfranchising qualified voters. The number of ballots you begin with is not necessarily the number that will be counted.

It is an administrative challenge to keep the records straight as the process unfolds.   That is why a methodology and training are required to ensure that every valid vote is counted properly. It's the only way to ensure a fair and impair election.

A typical election proceeded as follows. Once the meeting was brought to order, election monitors were introduced and given the floor – at which time we explained to the assembly the process we were going to follow. We then announced the qualifications to serve as a "volunteer impartial committee member." Next we picked volunteers from a show of hands. We had a standing rule known only to us. The rule was that anyone suggested by petitioners or by the association to serve on the impartial committee was automatically out of the running.

We usually picked two volunteers to work with one of our monitors, and thus to constitute a three-member team. Each monitor served as both team leader and ballot reader, while one volunteer acted as recorder for the association and the other volunteer as the recorder for the Ombudsman's Office. Once the volunteers were selected, they were checked against various lists of owners, the board of directors, officer and candidate lists and unit numbers to ensure they met the criteria. They were then asked to sign both volunteer sheets, indicating their assigned team for the record. Next, the ballot box was opened in the presence of the assembly and all envelopes were counted to confirm that the 20 percent voting requirement was met. The assembly was informed about the number of envelopes on hand and that the required 20 percent had been satisfied, as well as the percentage of participation. The 20 percent requirement was satisfied at every election we conducted.

Many people did not realize that the annual meeting actually combined two meetings – the business meeting and the election. In principle, you could have one without the other. If you had a quorum for the business meeting, you had a business meeting. If you had 20 percent voter participation, you had an election If you had both, they could take place simultaneously.

Once we had all the envelopes on the table, the committee members would put them in unit order. That made it easy to identify duplicates and deal with those first. The remaining envelopes were divided into equal parts to balance the load and to make it possible for all the teams to complete their tasks at about the same time. The authorized voter list was split up along those breakouts. Each team signed their respective portion of the list and used it to perform the outer envelope verification for their portion.

Each team now had their individual worksheet with the team members aware of their starting envelope number, i.e., their base number. We brought all necessary supplies to do the job – calculators, letter openers, staplers, scotch tape, black and red pens, paper clips, rubber bands, and yes, spare envelopes. We were self-sufficient, mobile voting machines. By the way, we never placed letter openers on the table before they were needed. Once an outer envelope is open, the polls are closed, and we didn't want that to happen prematurely. Volunteers were instructed on all task at an appropriate time in order to avoid possible mistakes. Teams proceeded to do outer envelope verification, checking off each ballot as a qualified vote.

If a disregard situation was encountered, the team reviewed the reason with the team leader. The team leader then reviewed it with the attorney, if one was present, before stamping it "disregarded," recording the reason on the worksheet and adjusting down the valid envelope count accordingly. Once the envelope verification was completed and the valid count adjusted, one final announcement was made to accept

Condo Board Election Revolt!

ballots before the polls were officially closed. We then counted the voter list check-off marks for "have voted" and compared this number to the number of outer envelopes. At that point an announcement was made regarding the number of valid outer envelopes.

We never entered into discussion on the disregarded envelopes. Unit owners could ask to review that information at a later date. Once stamped "disregarded" (with the reason recorded on the envelope), it was a done deal. We waited for all teams to complete the validation phase before proceeding to the next phase. Prior to opening the outer envelopes, our volunteers were instructed that if they found an outer envelope to contain anything but a ballot envelope, they were not to remove its contents but to give it to their team leader.

When envelopes included voter certificates, proxies or in some cases, ballots without envelopes, the team leader knew what to do and kept the process moving smoothly. Once all the outer envelopes were opened, each team did an outer to inner envelope count check to make sure we still had a one-for-one relationship and, if not, it had to be reconciled. For instance, an outer envelope could contain two ballots from an owner who owned two units, but used a single outer envelope. Such a situation also required adjustments to the authorized voting list indicating two units voted in the event it had not been identified on the outer envelope.

Condo Board Election Revolt!

All of these situations had to be monitored to retain correct records and counts.

The opened outer envelopes were bundled by teams with their identifier and number of envelopes in their bundles. The bundles and the disregarded, unopened outer envelopes were filed in the record retention box provided.

We were now ready to open the inner envelopes containing the ballots. Since we had no way to determine the contents of these envelopes in advance, volunteers were instructed to turn over any envelope containing anything but a single ballot to the team leader. For this phase of the election, the team leader would let the two volunteers open the envelopes. He would then perform a quick ballot scan for over-votes. If he found an over-vote, the team leader would show it to the two volunteers and then stamp it "disregarded as an over-vote." If the ballot was under-voted, the number of votes cast was recorded on the back of the ballot to prevent later tampering. It prevented someone adding some tick marks on one of these ballots to change the count and later challenge it, knowing it had been changed.

The monitor would then place the ballots face down in front of himself. Once all ballots were open, the ballots were counted – as were the inner envelopes – to confirm the one-for-one requirement. The inner envelopes were bundled, tagged with the count and team number, and filed in the retention box. Ballots were bundled in groups of 20 or 25 ballots. We had the final valid ballot count and informed the assembly of that number. Now everybody knew what we were down to.

After each group of ballots was counted, a check would be made and a different colored pen would be used for the next group of ballots being tallied. The team leader served as the reader, while the two volunteers sitting on either side of him recorded the tally, one for the association and the other for the Ombudsman's office.

Early in this game we found out that even if an association did everything right, the ballot reader could single-handedly change the result of the election if left to his own devices. For that reason, we election monitors were the readers. We made it a practice of holding the ballot face up, placing our finger on the cast vote and calling out who the vote was being cast for. That way the recorders on either side of the reader could visually see where his finger was on the ballot and so could the whole assembly. They recorded tallies in groups of five to facilitate counting.

Once the bundle of ballots was read and recorded, the team leader held that bundle while one recorder told the other the number of votes they had recorded for each candidate; if they agreed, they circled the number for the candidate. If for some reason they had a different

Condo Board Election Revolt!

number recorded for a given candidate, they took a separate piece of paper and re-recorded the tally for that candidate as the team leader redid the re-announced check of only that candidate.

The correction was made to the sheet that was in error. The recorders changed to the red pen for the next group of ballots. The process went on until all ballots were counted. The circled numbers were added up for each candidate and placed in the total column. Again, both sets of tally sheets were checked for identical totals. Team results were then transferred to a summary sheet, combining all team totals into a final count. The results were announced to the assembly. They were told how many votes each candidate received and who the winners were.

The association's set of tally sheets were placed in the record retention box along with the ballots. The custody of the box was turned over to the custodian in front of the assembly for the required one-year retention. To wrap things up on my end, I had fourteen days to draft the association's report.

For every election I conducted, I completed my report the next day. All my reports were filed and my files were closed within twenty-four hours. After the elections we often received standing ovations and many thanks. Many would say and report that the elections that we monitored were the most efficient and effective election process they had ever experienced. These comments came from attorneys, property managers, and board members. Our process did take longer than some at times. My take was after all the expense the membership had gone through to hold an election, now was not the time to skimp. Getting it right was the objective.

We never had a count challenged, because the numbers always tallied and the membership was able to **observe** the totals being developed. We had full confidence with 100% accuracy in the voting results we announced even when we had a one-vote difference between candidates. Unfortunately, we had no control of events that took place prior to the election itself. One could still make the case for GIGO (garbage in garbage out), due to events that took place before the election was conducted.

On more than one occasion we drove home wondering about pre-election events and reminding ourselves that we were just VCs, (Validators and Counters). I told myself, "We will make the best of this questionable election." It was hard at times to look into the disappointed faces that seemed to say, "What am I paying you for?"

Imagine that you had a long, frustrating problem with your association but were unable to convince even the Division to help resolve it. Suddenly, an intelligent person stood before you who responded to requests in

Condo Board Election Revolt!

a timely manner.   Wouldn't your hopes for a speedy resolution be raised? But now that person declares, "I can't help you. Contact the Division."

You would probably have the same discouraged look on your face. In the end, this was the canned bad news we had to deliver. At every election we attended, we entered a world of frustration and stress. You felt the pressure from all sides, but could not lose sight of the mission. You were there as the outside intruder, a forced fit, facing a well of resentment. Diplomacy was a must. Overall, perhaps we were not doing that bad a job, because as time went on even the Division started sending clients our way.

Chapter Eight
The Division

The duties and powers of the Division of Land Sales, Condominiums, and Mobile Homes are spelled out in Appendix G, if you're interested in the details.

I stated earlier that Dr. Rizzo was a bureau chief in his own right, appointed by the Governor and his job was defined by the Legislature. As with the Advisory Council On Condominiums, the Office of the Condominium Ombudsman was attached to the Division for administrative purposes only. Dr. Rizzo's staff members were not considered employees of the Division. They were employees of the Office of the Condominium Ombudsman, an important point to remember.

As a volunteer staff member attached to that same Office, on occasion I had a need to deal with issues related to the Division. Specifically, I will share some of the issues that dealt with my leg of the Ombudsman organizational chart: election monitoring. I'm certain a great deal went on related to Dr. Rizzo's other mandated arenas that I'm not aware of. I remember one incident that was not directly or specifically related to my responsibilities. It had to do with Virgil working from home. I don't know all the details.

Condo Board Election Revolt!

As I recall, Virgil told me that in mid-February 2006, the Division informed him that he had not yet obtained permission from the Division to work from home. Yet he had been working at his home 24/7 since Day One. Everybody knew that. This fact was not a new discovery. When he told me that the Division now wanted him to obtain permission to work at home, I started to laugh. Virgil asked me what was so funny? I said, "Well, now you know how unit owners feel. It only took the Division a-year-and-a-half to get around to asking. You're lucky. They could have followed up with that one a year or so after your departure."

Then there was the problem where mail at the Office of the Condominium Ombudsman had already been opened. I even received opened letters addressed to the "Condominium Ombudsman Election Monitor." It was obvious for whom that mail was intended. That went on for a while until Virgil had it. He filed a complaint with the Office of the Inspector General. That Office said it would investigate. I don't know what happened, because I departed right after that complaint was filed.

At times I felt that we were dealing with two different Divisions, the one in Tallahassee and the one in Fort Lauderdale. I had a good relationship with the Bureau of Enforcement staff at our Office. I had the opportunity to work closely with them. On occasion they recommended the unit owners petition us to help with their election problems.

Condo Board Election Revolt!

We also helped the Ft. Lauderdale office close some very old election complaints, as well as some recent ones. On a couple occasions the Tallahassee office even requested that we conduct elections at some problem facilities, indicating that we could work together if we respected each other's turf. Early in the game it had been made clear to us that the Division was intent upon clarifying the meaning of the "Conduct Election" wording of the statute. To me, it was like Bill Clinton and the definition of "sex." I knew what "conduct" meant. Perhaps the opposition did not like the inherent meaning of "conduct," but I can't speak for them.

My first involvement with the Division in Tallahassee was over the change to the election monitor FAC rule (section 61B-23.00215). Every now and then an opportunity presents itself to change one rule or other. Basically, this is how it works. The Division selects a section of the rule for change, makes the change, and posts the hearing notice. The hearing is held, the notice of change runs for 21 days, and the rule is filed for adoption; then in another 21 days it may or may not be adopted. Close enough for my purpose here.

I recall three times when the FAC rule change affected election monitoring. The first instance occurred in May 2005 when Dr. Rizzo requested a teleconference to provide his input to proposed rule change 61B-23.00215. During the conference call for that hearing, Dr. Rizzo requested many changes to that section of the FAC.

Condo Board Election Revolt!

(Remember, this was one of the Ombudsman's duties, as defined by the 2004 Florida Legislature.) NONE of his suggested changes made it into the rule change. The Ombudsman was off to a good start on this one, batting zero. An omen of things to come. I remember one specific change we wanted. It had to do with run-off elections. For those of you unfamiliar with the term, a run-off election is required during the regular election when two or more candidates tie for the remaining director positions. The way the rule still reads is that election monitors cannot conduct run-off elections.

We wanted wording changed in the rule to state "except for petitioned elections." That way we could finish the job if we were asked to do so by the petitioners as an extension of the original petition. Although this would have been a sensible and logical rule change, the Division failed to make the change. We had a half dozen petitioned elections that ended with a run-off election requirement. In each instance we were asked to **conduct** the run-off election, but we had to refuse. When asked why we were not coming back to finish the job, we had to inform the requesters (sometimes the petitioners and sometimes the association), that the rule did not permit us to do so.

That was our first attempt to change the Florida Administrative Code. To repeat, NONE of Dr. Rizzo's many proposed changes made it into the rule change, as starkly revealed at the Miami Advisory Council On

Condo Board Election Revolt!

Condominiums meetings later that year. I was sitting near Representative Robaina and told him that none of our recommended changes had made in the final draft that I was reviewing. He was furious and chastised the Division for not working with the Ombudsman.

Dr. Rizzo had his first meeting with the new DBPR Secretary in September 2005. At that meeting, the Secretary attacked the function of the election monitor program as being contrary to the present control of the election process of the Division. You bet it was and by legislative mandate no less. Yet, that fact did not seem to matter to the Secretary.

In the presence of Dr. Rizzo, she immediately ordered her assistant "to effectuate a change in the Administrative Rule to limit the Ombudsman and election monitors to passive status." She apparently did not care what the statute required and who was giving the marching orders. Lo and behold, in January 2006 a notice of FAC rule change for Section 61B-23.00215 was posted. Not bad. It only took four months for that direct order from the DBPR Secretary to her aide to be implemented. The change was to strike out the wording **conduct** election and replace it with **observe**. This change was in direct conflict with the statute and the legislature's intentions when the statute was created. It didn't stay posted for long.

Condo Board Election Revolt!

That attempt at changing the FAC backfired and brought on a storm of protest from all quarters. Initially, the DBPR denied such a notice was been posted. The notice was rapidly removed, then acknowledged as posted, but explained as a concept that was only in the pipeline and not yet approved for change! The third FAC rule change notice, again affecting 61B-23.00215, appeared in April 2006 just before I "retired" as a volunteer. I provided input to that rule change hearing, but have no idea what effect it had. If the other input attempts were any indication, I suspect it had very little impact on the proposed rule change.

Why did we bother if our inputs were ignored? The answer was simple. The rule was an effective place to bring about operational change without having to write new law. It was far easier to change the rule than it was to change the statute. Dr. Rizzo viewed this as the way to bring about needed change and to correct operating deficiencies quickly. So did the Division apparently. Guess who's changes won out?

We put a lot of time and energy into preparing our input to the rule change hearings, batting zero each time. That was frustrating, because it was time wasted that could have been more effectively channeled to other enterprises. As a volunteer staff member, I had the occasion to sit in on several of Virgil's staff meetings. I remember one particular meeting where the DBPR Assistant Deputy Director met the staff for the first time. I had a disagreement with her when she insisted that boards of directors had to conduct the elections for their associations and could not farm out the duty. I told her they could and did so all the time. Property managers and attorneys frequently did so; they even conducted election themselves.

She said she would have to see that authority. I told her that I would send her the information that allowed boards to assign agents to conduct elections and to perform other business for the association. After the meeting Virgil said, "You didn't let her off the hook, did you?" I said, "Right, and these are the people that want to achieve better understanding of the meaning of how to conduct the elections." Now I understand why. As soon as I reached home, I pulled out the books and sent the information to Virgil in an e-mail that he could forward to the deputy.

My next experience with the Division also led me to further question what type of people were in charge. We had a fully validated election where the attorney for the association was challenging our qualifications to conduct the election. (Had he bothered to check with other attorneys from his law firm who had been at prior elections we held, he would have had the answer. That would have taken care of that issue.) Next he challenged the number of monitors assigned, the travel time, the mileage cost, and the estimated duration. The association posted a notice stating that we would not be allowed to conduct the election if they did receive satisfactory answers to all of questions raised. As I saw it, what we charged was no more of the attorney's business than what he charged was ours.

To make a long story short, this issue made its way up to the Legislative and the DBPR Secretary level, as it should have. The Secretary agreed with the Legislator and instructed the Division Director to contact the attorney, instructing him to "educate" that association attorney. In short, to read him the riot act. Obviously, the Director did not do that because initially we were still denied access to the election as promised. In addition, the attorney apparently convinced the Director that his invoice inquiry had merit. Now the Director was making inquiries into that matter – jumping with both feet into the neighbor's pool again.

At the election, I found out that the matter had been elevated to charges of alleged wrongdoing on the part of the Ombudsman as it related to monitor payment. I warned that attorney that he was making unfounded, serious, and slanderous charges and if the Director shared those views that the Ombudsman would set him straight. Apparently, that didn't happen either.

The invoice issue took on a life of its own and I suspect it played a major role in Dr. Rizzo's discharge. We know the Division did not do its homework because of later published reasons for Dr. Rizzo's dismissal. Again, all of this occurred because a subordinate failed to follow his superior's instructions. That's how I see it.

Let me bring all this together for you. In Chapter 3, Challenge #3, the issue of monitor payment, we were scratching our heads on how to get the monitors paid. We knew that Section 61B-23.00215(8) of the rule basically stated that the Division would not ensure that monitors were paid if the association failed to do so. They could have left that tidbit out of the rule because it was a given. We asked them to remove it, because we saw it as a red flag that could unnecessarily complicate payment as was the case.

Under these conditions, the provision in 61B-23.00215(9) made sense and was needed. If you want to be paid, you must receive part or all of your payment up front. As you'll see, that didn't always work either. But at least we had something to go by. So we decided to request payment five days in advance of the election. On the challenged invoice I referred to earlier, we provided instructions to make the check payable to the Condominium Election Monitor and to send it to the Condominium Ombudsman Election Monitor post office box five days before the scheduled election.

The check was finally received ninety days after the election, despite the fact that it had been cut six days before the election. The check should have been available election night, but only after the association received a final notice of overdue payment did they finally pay. I'll let you guess on whose orders payment had been withheld all that time.

Back to Challenge #3. If we were to have several volunteer monitors attend a single election, it would not be practical to have the association cut checks for each of them. What if the association refused to pay as it did in the situation above? What would the monitors do? Who would keep track of claims of payment or non-payment by the monitors? It was a sure way of losing the volunteers if they went through all the effort to become a monitor, making all the adjustments necessary to be available on demand, and were then stiffed for all their effort. We could not let that happen.

There was only one solution. Someone had to serve as the focal point to ensure payment. Guess who? We felt the associations should write a single check and send it to a single place. Once that check was received and cleared, individual checks would be cut to pay the monitors. I agreed to serve as that reference point and conduit. I say conduit because, as indicated, I did not want a business but recognized that it had to be run like a business.

So we started having the checks made payable to me personally, but that made it look like I was receiving all that money – which was clearly unacceptable from my point of view. There had to be a better way. To correct the situation, I established a second personal checking account with the pseudo name of Condominium Election Monitor – the same title that is on my County and City Election Monitor license. It was solely my account. Dr. Rizzo had absolutely no access to the checkbook, he never wrote a check, he never received a bank statement, and he never exercised oversight – because I kept him posted every time monitors were paid.

In a Miami Herald article, a spokesperson for the State claimed that one of the reasons for Dr. Rizzo's dismissal was that he had set up a private bank account to pay for condo election monitors, contrary to administrative rules. As you can see, the spokesperson was ill informed. Why are you giving me so much detail, you ask? Because it is very important. So I'll repeat it. One of the allegations given for Dr. Rizzo's dismissal was that he opened a checking account to pay the monitors. The accusation links back, no doubt, to the attorney's complaint I alluded to earlier. Dr. Rizzo never opened a checking account to pay monitors. This totally erroneous accusation implied financial wrongdoing, a rather serious error on their part and a reputation-damaging defamation charge on the other, as I see it. This accusation was made by a spokesman for the DBPR, not by the Governor.

We're not done yet; there is more. Remember the mailing instructions on the invoice. Well, that Post

Condo Board Election Revolt!

Office Box was mine. It was opened by me, paid by me, and closed by me. Dr. Rizzo never had a key to access that box. If it weren't mine, how would I have been permitted to close it? The box was in the name of Condominium Ombudsman Election Monitor – my title and not the Ombudsman's. Nevertheless, a further allegation appeared in print that he opened a post office box for the purpose ensuring that payments were sent directly to him. In my view, this lie cast more doubt on Dr. Rizzo's character. Perhaps the attorney referred to previously had convinced the Director to buy his line of thinking, hook, line, and sinker. Regardless of the source, it was a total fabrication.

The DBPR's stated reasons for Virgil's dismissal were different than those stated by the Governor. According to the Governor, Virgil was dismissed for failing to follow the "rules of engagement." How could the Governor expect the rules of engagement to be followed when he never met with Virgil to discuss them from the start – much less when he first heard that Virgil was not following the rules of engagement. As I see it, the Governor's failure to communicate the "rules of engagement" to the Ombudsman made him part of the problem. The Governor abdicated his duty to directly supervise, assist, and communicate with the Ombudsman. As the old saying goes, "You're either part of the solution or your part of the problem." I leave it to the reader to decide where the blame really lies.

Condo Board Election Revolt!

Now let's talk about the next questionable Division action, as it relates to the request for all of our 2005 election records, indeed, all 2424 pages of them. When I heard about the request, the first thing that came to mind was, "Why does an attorney for one law firm want the records of elections that he/she had nothing to do with? Why does he/she need all those petitioner names in his/her possession?" I know they are public records, but can you imagine someone making the same request of the Division.

The Advisory Council on Condominiums (ACC): As of June 30th of 2006, the ACC failed to publish eight page reports for the January, April and May meeting minutes. Six months later we were still waiting for them. Yet, the Ombudsman had to cough up all his election records for a whole year. (Yes, while this one-man band was out on sick leave, he was badgered by the Division's request.) By the way, the Division has no provision for recognizing sick leave as a valid reason for non-compliance. Hello! Perhaps this works for a 144-person organization, but hardly for a Lone Ranger. There should have been some leeway.

Here is the normal process for obtaining public records from the Division, as it was explained to me. An individual makes a request. The affected office is notified and asked to provide information on the cost. The applicant is so informed. When th check is received, it is deposited in the fund and the office

Condo Board Election Revolt!

involved is notified and has ten days to provide the record. Usually it's one or two reports requested. If it's a large number, you have more time to respond. How much is large? Who knows? How much longer do you have to fill the order? Who knows?

In this case, the cost was over $400, and the Division lost the check. A fax copy of the check was provided, but you can't cash a fax. First the Division said, "We have the check." Then the Division said, "No, you have the check." Then they admitted the check was lost, but instructions came down to fill the order anyway. Why? I suspect it was because of who the requestor was, or the impact such a huge request would make on the strained resources, or because the man was on his back and could not do it. Answer: Probably all of the above.

I don't know if the check was ever found, if a new check was provided, or if Florida Condo Owners ended up paying for that expensive record request. The order was finally filled through hard work and sacrifice – without overtime pay – all the while keeping other work on schedule. I have a theory and it's this. If you have a small, efficient work group and want to kill their efficiency, bog them down in administration. It was a brilliant strategy. I have to take my hat off to them, but it didn't work that time. On the day the materials were shipped, within hours after the mailing, the requester sued the Division and the Ombudsman for failing to provide the requested documents on time. Guess what?

Condo Board Election Revolt!

Now the Division attorneys needed a copy of these same 2424 pages! Deja vu all over again.

The Ombudsman was now informed that he would have to pay the other party's legal fees out of his budget (the Condo Owners' trust fund). The boss was on sick leave and there was no petty cash to pay for the mailing due to the missing check. This created an immediate cash flow need. The Chief Election Monitor to the rescue. I paid for the mailings from my monitor proceeds.

Then came the last bureaucratic straw. A memo from the Division in Tallahassee instructed the Ombudsman's Office to plan better, because it was way over the monthly projections for copying supplies and related costs. Khrushchev said, "We will destroy you from within." Do you think somebody read his play book?
I told you I would be discussing Division Enforcement. So here we are. I stated that there is no behavior change if there is no consequence. That axiom is proven in spades when it comes to condominium associations. Poor behavior is unlikely to change until individual offenders pay the consequence. Forcing association members to pay fines for offenses committed against fellow members is insane. If the Division took punitive action against the real offenders that provide the advice – attorneys and CAMs – owners would not have to pay special assessments stemming from Division fines on an association. What a novel idea..

Condo Board Election Revolt!

Here is the Division's position on enforcement, right out of the book. See Appendix E: "The division recognizes that unit owner controlled associations are comprised of volunteer members who, in most circumstances, are lay people without specialized knowledge of the complex statutory and administrative rule structure of Chapter 718, F.S. Based upon this understanding, the division, as set forth in these rules, will first and foremost attempt to seek statutory and rule compliance through an educational resolution.

For repeated statutory or rule violations by board members, where the violations have not been corrected or otherwise resolved by the association, the division will seek statutory or rule compliance through an enforcement resolution." The Division tells you the reason why it doesn't levy fines on board members, but it fails to put changes in place to fix this flaw. The question the Division should ask itself is: "When are we doing to put in place mechanisms necessary to punish the guilty without punishing the victims?" I am unaware of any undertaking by the Division along those lines.

The next argument you will hear from the Division is: "Even if we attempt to enforce compliance with our rules, no one will volunteer to do the job." My take on that is: It's a sad day for association members if volunteers are the only people you can find to force board members to perform their fiduciary responsibility. Moreover, that theory has not been tested. Who knows if volunteers will or will not sign up? Maybe the same bad apples will continue to run for office, but at least they will be on notice that they their wings could be clipped if they don't change their behavior. And perhaps they will turn a new leaf and perform their job within appropriate legal parameters. Appendix E details the Division's authority and places a number of tools at the Division's disposal to correct election wrongdoing.

Condo Board Election Revolt!

Chapter Nine
Advisory Council on Condominiums

Florida Statute 718.50151 defines the role of the Advisory Council on Condominiums (ACC). (See Appendix F.) What is the role of the Council? The Attorney General spelled it out in one of his Advisory Opinions (AGO 2005-18), a portion of which is printed below.

It reads the same as the statute. I think it is clear what the ACC's job was and still is. The excerpt from the Attorney General's opinion reads: "In 2004, the Florida Legislature created the Advisory Council on Condominiums.[1] Pursuant to section 718.50151(1), Florida Statutes, the council is made up of seven appointed members: two appointed by the President of the Senate, two appointed by the Speaker of the House of Representatives, and three appointed by the Governor. The Director of the Division of Florida Land Sales, Condominiums, and Mobile Homes (Division) of the Department of Business and Professional Regulation serves as an ex officio nonvoting member. The council is located within the Division for administrative purposes. Council members serve without compensation but are entitled to receive per diem and travel expenses pursuant to section 112.061, Florida

Condo Board Election Revolt!

Statutes, while they are conducting official business." Section 718.50151(2), Florida Statutes, provides that the functions of the Advisory Council are to: "(a) Receive, from the public, input regarding issues of concern with respect to condominiums and recommendations for changes in the condominium law. The issues that the council shall consider include, but are not limited to, the rights and responsibilities of the unit owners in relation to the rights and responsibilities of the association. (b) Review, evaluate, and advise the Division concerning revisions and adoption of rules affecting condominiums. (c) Recommend improvements, if needed, in the education programs offered by the Division."

Looking at the Attorney General's statement that the Council and the Office of the Condominium Ombudsman are both located within the Division for administrative purposes, leads me to ask, "Why wasn't the Council micromanaged as well?" From what I saw and heard, the Division did not try to micromanage the Council. Was it because an active member of the Division served on the Council?

In fact, this legal opinion focused on whether or not meetings between that Division member and the members of the Council were subject to the Sunshine Law. The Attorney General ruled the Council members were subject to the Sunshine Law, when he said that notices, public accessibility, and written minutes apply to any meeting where two or more members of the Council discuss matters on which it can be foreseen that the board may take action.

Why, as of July 2006, were there no reported minutes for the three Council meetings already held during 2006? The same Division employee who so vigorously kept after the Ombudsman to cough up a year's worth of election records attended these meetings. It appears we have a dual standard here. If the Division and the ACC had to provide all their records for a year's worth of activity, as Dr. Rizzo had to do, I wonder what those records would reveal? I feel that Khrushchev "from within" theory resurfacing in my mind. Let's take a close look at the three areas the Council is supposed to focus on:

1. Receive, from the public, input regarding issues of concern with respect to condominiums and recommendations for changes in the condominium law.

2. Review, evaluate, and advise the Division concerning revisions and adoption of rules affecting condominiums.

3. Recommend improvements, if needed, in the education programs offered by the Division.

Do you see anything listed above about riding herd over the Office of the Condominium Ombudsman? I attended three Council's meeting in 2005. Much of the Council's time was devoted to the subject of the Ombudsman Office. At one meeting I attended, ACC members spent so much time on that topic that they had little time to accept comments from the unit owners in attendance, which is the priority task mandated to them by the Legislature. Remember their three areas of responsibility. The Council was writing meeting reports back in 2005. Perhaps they had something they wanted the public to read. You can access the ACC reports online at MyFlorida.com. Here is the direct link:

http://www.state.fl.us/dbpr/lsc/condominiums/advisory_council/index.shtml

From Day One, the Council demanded to be kept informed about the names of monitors and their qualifications, as if it was any of their business. We were asked to show up at the two-day Miami meeting in order to put this subject to bed once and for all. After some introductory remarks, Dr. Rizzo said to the Council, "You've been wanting to know all about my volunteers. I'm going to let them tell you all about themselves and you can ask them your questions directly." With those words he handed me the microphone. I began to say my name, but never got it out before the Chairman said, "We really don't have time for that now, we need to move on to other business." That was it. The subject never came up again.

Condo Board Election Revolt!

As I said before, later at that same meeting the Division representative reported that the election monitor rule had been updated and handed out copies. The vice chairman asked Virgil if his input had been added. I was reading the document; Virgil had not yet seen it. Virgil glanced at me and I shook my head indicating "no." Again, I touched on this point earlier. I was sitting next to Representative Julio Robaina and told him that our inputs had not been accepted and that the marked up version we used during the conference call was at my home. "Send it to me," he said. Then he stood up and addressed his concern over the lack of cooperation.

My last experience with the Council was when I attended the Orlando meeting. The attacks on the Office of the Condominium Ombudsman at that meeting were so fierce that I finally got up and left when the Chair said, **"What are we going to do about this 500-pound gorilla in our living room that no one seems to want to talk about?"** By the way, I recorded that whole meeting.

Little did I know that the gorilla would become our mascot. I had a small gorilla with red boxing gloves that I still have on my shelf. I made a small sign for it "Virgil The Ombudsman" and tacked it on its chest with Velcro. I took a picture of it and framed it in an 8x10 frame. Virgil had this picture on his desk at work. As far as I know, that is the only item he removed from his Office after the dismissal. It's also appears on this book cover.

Condo Board Election Revolt!

That's the light side of it. The serious side is the view that the Council took of the Office of the Ombudsman from the outset and the amount of time and effort the ACC put into undermining the Office. If you check the statute, the Division, the ACC, and the Office of the Condominium Ombudsman had the following areas of overlap responsibility:

1. Education
2. FAC Changes
3. Unit Owner Complaints
4. Reporting

However, only one of these three entities was required by statute to Conduct Elections – the Office of the Condominium Ombudsman. Yet the other two entities spent a major amount of their time on an activity that was not within their purview. Nor was the role of the Ombudsman for that matter, but that did not stop them. I have my own opinion: "Conduct Elections" was the only provision in the statute with real authority. It not only worked, but hurt the bad guys and they wanted to put a stop to it.

There was a great deal of "pleading" in the background to get the 500-pound gorilla under control. Tranquilizers would not do, they had to kill it and finally did. The three entities could not work together on important common issues. Let's take a closer look at areas of overlapping responsibility, starting with education. The Division gave Community Associations Institute a $500,000 education contract without involving the Ombudsman in the decision, even though he shares that education responsibility with the Division. Nor did they allocate any funds for his educational requirement use. He was forced to support his education programs through individuals that offered to help at no charge. I do not recall the ACC and the Division working with Dr. Rizzo on education. I do remember his running into problems when he did set out on his own to establish education programs.

The next common area: FAC changes. Again, I don't remember the ACC working with Dr. Rizzo on the FAC. We already know how the Division dealt with Dr. Rizzo's FAC change recommendations. As to the unit owner complaint responsibility, I always felt the ACC should have and could have dedicated more time to hearing from unit owners and less time scrutinizing the Office of the Condominium Ombudsman. Several Council members also shared that view.

A quick look at reporting: We already know that the ACC with its Division (ex officio member) has not yet written any of its reports for their three meetings held in 2006. I can tell you that Dr. Rizzo's quarterly reports raised all kinds of hell. Also, from those reports came the records request I discussed in Chapter 9. In the 2005 Fourth Quarter Report, we reported having conducted 43 elections during 2005. Once this information was

Condo Board Election Revolt!

made known, those 2424 pages of information were soon requested. As far as legislative activity, if you check the ACC's year-end report, you'll find the Council found something wrong with all of the fifteen statute changes recommended by the Ombudsman.

I want to share a fascinating excerpt from the ACC year-end report: "By and large the majority of the public input indicates that there are no unique or emerging issues regarding condominium living or the quality of life in this type of living arrangement. Indeed, the concerns expressed by the public do not differ substantially from those expressed to the 1991 Condominium Study Commission created by the 1990 Legislature or to the 1996 Division of Florida Land Sales, Condominiums and Mobile Homes Study, commissioned by the 1995 Legislature. Consistent with the Division of Florida Land Sales, Condominiums and Mobile Homes quarterly report to the Legislature, public testimony from unit owners generally dealt with issues involved with everyday condominium living. Those who voiced complaints generally had issues with the way their elections were conducted, access to records, problems working with their board of directors, or financial issues.

However, these complaints viewed in their totality do not suggest to the Council, as a general matter, that there are serious problems with respect to the quality of condominium living in Florida. Indeed, as a matter of course, with over 19,000 residential condominium associations, there will always be those unit owners who didn't get access to records in a timely manner, an election, which malfunctions, or a board that doesn't do a good job managing the condominium's fiscal affairs. However, the Council believes such occurrences are the exception and not the rule. Moreover, as one might logically conclude, the bulk of these concerns emanate from Broward, Miami-Dade, and Palm Beach Counties, where most of Florida's condominium population is located."

I agree with the report that the bulk of the problems are in Broward, Miami-Dade, and Palm Beach counties. That is where 90 percent of all the elections I was involved in took place. I disagree with the Council when it claims there are no serious problems with respect to quality of life. The ACC members didn't look into the eyes of desperate and disenchanted owners. Had the ACC spent more time listening to owners instead of dissecting the Office of the Condominium Ombudsman, it may have arrived at a different conclusion. Though only a volunteer, I probably received more input from unit owners than the Council did at all of its meetings. And this was only the tip of the complaint iceberg when one considers all the complaints received by the Office of the Condominium Ombudsman.

Condo Board Election Revolt!

The ACC's report goes on to say: "More importantly, in the context of the Council's receipt of the foregoing public testimony and subsequent discussion, the Council has identified eleven specific recommendations, some of which will require legislative action. The most important of these concern enhancement of educational opportunities for unit owners and board members, the role of the Ombudsman, post turnover jurisdiction of condominiums, and emergency board powers.

In sum, the Division needs to expand educational opportunities and request necessary appropriations if warranted. The legislature needs to clarify the role of the Ombudsman and emphasize his or her role as a neutral liaison rather than an enforcer of condominium law, and provide specific powers rather than the plenary æall powers necessary' language of the present law."

The Ombudsman was the ACC's focus, yes, even its obsession. I know because I was there or was involved in follow-ups for at least half of the ACC's meetings in 2005 – when they had a lot to say about the Ombudsman. Don't take my word for it. You can determine that for yourself if you're so inclined. Just go online and read the ACC's 2005 meeting reports. Looking back on all of this, who do you think was really out of bounds? Was it the Ombudsman or the ACC and the Division? You decide. In any event, I rest my case.

Chapter Ten
Election Experiences

You may find some of the experiences that I'm sharing with you unbelievable. I submit to you every story is true. They all happened. Nobody could make this much up. Sometimes they didn't want us there. After you read all this, you'll understand why. Everybody likes to make fun of his or her boss. I'm no exception, so what better way to start these anecdotes than with him. After all, this book is all about Dr. Rizzo. Here goes:

Where is the Envelope? At one election, completing the outer envelope verification phase of the election and doing our count check, we came up one short. We checked the table, looked on the floor. No envelope to be found. I looked over to Dr. Rizzo who was standing in the audience deep in conversation. I noticed an envelope in the breast pocket of his shirt. I went up to him and asked, "Is that what I think it is?" "Yes," he replied, "We have to resolve this one before we start opening the envelopes." Mystery solved. We'd had an earlier question on this envelope but the attorney had not yet arrived. Dr. Rizzo was holding it to discuss it with the attorney. From then on, whenever we had a count discrepancy – whether or not Virgil was present – the standing joke was, "Where is Virgil? We need to check his pockets."

Condo Board Election Revolt!

The Electric Letter Opener. Then there was the time when we were testing new tools to speed up the election process. We were employing new battery-operated palm letter openers. To use them effectively, you needed to tap the envelope on end and cut the other narrow end. Virgil did not tap the envelope and cut it along the long end. He ended up with a two-piece ballot. Scotch tape to the rescue and the end of that tool.

Parking Offense. When we arrived for the election, we were fortunate to find a guest parking spot right next to the clubhouse. The monitor backed into the slot in full view of the members arriving for the election. Following the election, we found a parking ticket on the windshield. The offense: the car was not facing forward in the slot. There had been a clean sweep of the board that night. When we brought the ticket to the new president, he told us that he would take care of it. Rank has its privilege.

Cost Effectiveness. Associations occasionally sent second-notice packages without the ballot or without voting envelopes.

Nobody is Perfect. Election notices had incorrect election dates, times, or places.

Where is the election? We had elections in all sorts of places. We had them in ballrooms, recreation rooms, and meeting rooms – all types of rooms. We had them by the pool. We even held one on a patio using the water fountain for both a seat and as the table for our work.

Flush with Facilities. Elections were held at the library, at town hall, and in small offices of property managers. Once we had one on the hood of a car in a dark parking lot, using flashlights and car headlights. Sometimes we were offered facilities that we had to refuse. At one election, I asked where I should set up, the president told me I could conduct the election in the men's room for all she cared. I told her the statute would not allow me to conduct it in the men's room, because she could not observe the proceedings.

Find the Election. At the last minute – well, not the last minute, actually one hour before the election – the election location was changed and a note was taped by the elevator. No, it wasn't moved to another room. It moved miles away. Fortunately, as was the rule, we tried to arrive early. This time it paid off. We arrived to find an agitated petitioner waiting for us at the entrance, pointing to cars that were departing. The board of directors and the election staff were leaving for the new election location. We followed them and conducted the election. Our presence was a surprise. Remember, while there were so many issues that could have been raised about this process, we only had authority to conduct the election and we did.

Condo Board Election Revolt!

No Election Here. This one had a different twist. When we arrived for the election, the maintenance man informed us there was no election that day. I showed him the association's election notice. He said he should know because he was responsible for setting up the room. He suggested that it might be at a section across the way. We walked over to the second meeting hall. Opening the door, we saw that a mahjong tournament was about to begin. We returned to the original meeting hall. But this time we opened the door. The board of directors was sitting at a table on the stage, while the property manager and his staff were at a table below the stage. We introduced ourselves. The meeting was turned over to us, and we conducted the election.

Lock the Door. This election was the exact opposite. Once we arrived, they locked the door behind us. No one else was able to enter. When I asked why the individual was locking the door, he replied, "Now no one else can vote. The polls were now closed." I said, "I don't think so. Besides, don't you think the fire marshal would object to you doing that with a room full of people?" The polls and the locked doors were reopened.

Empty Room Election. The election took place in a small crowded room with no chairs or tables. A unit owner brought a folding card table from his apartment. The attorney and three property management staff arrived fifteen minutes late. We conducted the election on this single card table with fifty onlookers.

Condo Board Election Revolt!

Musical Chairs. On several occasions we had jam-packed election rooms with never enough chairs. Unit owners would come in and take the chairs set aside for us at the election table, and we would have to send someone after them to return the chairs. We smartened up, picked a volunteer and posted him on guard duty to watch over our chairs while we were collecting ballots and handing out ballots to individuals voting in person.

Thanks Anyway. We received a petition request on which I had to rush to make the cut-off deadline for the notice. I worked on it over a holiday weekend. On Tuesday, the first workday of that week, I tried to contact the petitioner to inform him that his petition was validated and the notice was being drafted. He was not in so I left a voice mail asking him to call me. The next day passed, and I still had not heard from him. I finally was successful contacting him at home that evening. As soon as he heard my voice, he said he was going to call me to let me know they didn't need our services because they had an equal number of candidate and vacancies. He thanked me and hung up. I swallowed that one as I did several others that never made it to election phase for one reason or another.

Short Notice. A petitioner called to inquire how to request that we conduct the election. He wanted to know how to expedite the process. "When is your election scheduled for?" I asked. "Tonight," he replied.

Condo Board Election Revolt!

No Election. We processed a petition and had the election date set. When we arrived to conduct the election, we were informed that the election had already been held. They only wanted us there to observe the organizational meeting. The request had been made at the suggestion of a Division staff member.

Max Security. We also dealt with dramatic statements. At one election there was a three-foot square ballot box with a master lock. It sat on top of a table in the front of the roomful of people. The meeting was called to order, and we were introduced. Then this large, burly man walked in with three-foot long bolt cutters in his hands. On the president's command, he proceeded to cut the lock off the ballot box. I asked the president, "Don't you have a key?" He didn't answer me.

Simplicity. One small association had a shoe box with a removable top as their ballot box. It wasn't even taped shut.

Easy Access. The ballot box kept in the office had a slot large enough to put your hand in the box.

The Extremes. One association would not let you put a ballot in the box; they would do it for you, after you signed in. At another facility the ballot box sat in the middle of a busy lobby accessible to all and left unattended. Some used the mail slot at the office.

Condo Board Election Revolt!

Give it to Me or Stay Out. At one facility, unit owners who wished to hand their ballots directly to us were not permitted to come in unless they first handed their ballot through the door. We escorted them in.

Open Them Now. An assistant to the property manager stood at the entrance to the door, instructing voters to remove their ballot from the outer envelope and put it in the box just inside the entrance. We sent her packing.

Sign to Vote. I was getting ready to start the election and asked the secretary for the voter list. She said, "You can't have it yet. They are still signing in." I assumed she was using the voter list as many associations do. But no, the sign-in sheet was going to be my voter list. "How do you plan to work that?" I asked her. She replied, "If they didn't sign in, they're not voting." Thank God I had my property appraiser list with me.

Don't Sign It. Unit owners were giving us unsigned outer envelopes. When asked to sign them they replied, "We were told not to." Had they put their unsigned envelopes in the ballot box and left, their votes would not have been counted. A quick announcement put an end to that one.

No Spare Parts. On several occasions they did not have spare ballots and/or voting envelopes available. Bring your own. So we did.

Condo Board Election Revolt!

Who Votes? No association voter list. Property Appraiser list to the rescue once again.

CAM Manager Election Expert. (with 30 years of experience). "Where does it say in the rule I have to provide ballots at the election?" he asked.

Time-Out Corner. When we asked where we were going to do the election? "Go in that office," was the reply. "We can't do that," was my reply. "Then if you need to do this election in front of the membership, there's a table in the back of the room you can work there. Have at it." "But it's not in front of the membership." "Close enough," was the reply.

The Shredder. They opened the outer envelopes and put the ballots in the box. Where are the outer envelopes? They're shredded.

Who is in Charge? The property manager is running the meeting. Soon after we arrived, we learned that the president and vice president were sitting in the audience. When I asked the president why the board was not holding the meeting, she replied, "He always runs the show." What's wrong with this picture?

CAM Rules. Property manager and staff want to serve as the impartial committee. Why? We always done so. Not tonight!

Condo Board Election Revolt!

Who is Running this Place? It turned out that none of board members were owners, yet the Bylaws required ownership.

You Want Meetings; We Have Meetings. The problem was the president conducted them in Spanish without translation and the community spoke English. He kicked off the election with announcements in Spanish, then sat at the table and reached in the box to take a handful of ballots. My assistants spoke Spanish. We started the process again with instructions in English. The president took a seat in the audience until his term expired two hours later.

Voting Instructions. One voting instruction read: "Put your new voter certificate in with the ballot." Another read: "Put your ballot in the proxy envelope."

Bring in the Police. Often-time, police were present. They were never forced to use their authority and always left once they saw that we had it under control.

Vote for Us. Incumbents were listed first on the ballot, or worse yet, an incumbent bio was printed on the ballot.

What's the Difference? Illegal candidates were listed on the ballot or legal candidates were left off the ballot.

Condo Board Election Revolt!

I Was Late. First ballot goes out without the president's name on the ballot: "6 candidates, vote for 5." A couple days later, the president mails a new ballot: "7 candidates, vote for 1." We show up for the election before the dual ballot headache starts and common sense prevails. How was it resolved? The president and another candidate withdrew from the race. No election needed. All's well that ends well.

Selective Discard. Ballots that did not meet the property manager's acceptance criteria were trashed.

Dead Vote. A person who had been dead for several years was still being allowed to vote. And you were worried about not having a voter certificate on file.

Need the Deed. One association's voting records were so screwed up that we finally had to pull every deed in order to update the unit owner list.

Willed Property. I thought that someone finally appreciated all that I was doing for Florida condo owners. When I opened the outer envelope at this election, I found that it contained a will – nothing else – in the envelope. When I saw that the condo was not left to me, I was disappointed, so I put it back in the envelope, resealed it, and gave it to the attorney.

Condo Board Election Revolt!

Take it Back. Then there was the protest submission where all the second-notice material, including the unused ballot, was stuffed in the outer envelope and returned.

Fear of Death. A young lady's ballot was rejected because she had improperly prepared the voting materials sent to her by her mother, who was the owner. Upon finding out her ballot was disregarded, she came back to the meeting room to plead her case. Discovering that it was too late to do so, she was genuinely concerned. She said her mother was going to kill her when she found out she had messed up. One sympathetic monitor replied, "If you don't want to die, don't tell her."

Stacking the Deck. An incumbent director's wife once tried to sneak on the impartial committee and the spouse of a candidate also tried to do the same. They didn't make it. I compared their unit numbers to the property appraiser list, corporate filing, and the ballot before I accepted them. Nice try.

Vote for Me. A unit owner hands all her voting materials, including a blank ballot, to a member of the board sitting at the director's table in front of me. She tells him to fill out the ballot for her. She turns and starts to leave, while the director begins to filling out the ballot. I ask, "What do you think you're doing?" to which he replies, "Right," and goes chasing after the

Condo Board Election Revolt!

woman. He soon returns with her sealed ballot, smiles and says, "She voted herself. I'm sorry. I wasn't thinking." Do you want to bet how she voted?

Dual-Purpose Ballot. Ballots had listed candidates on the top half and issues to be voted on during the business meeting on the bottom. This ballot was governed by two different sets of voting rules, and the bottom half was necessary to establish the quorum for the business meeting. The association, however, would not have access to the ballot until after we had finished the election. By meeting with the property manager ahead of time, we were able to work out the mechanics of both elections to our mutual satisfaction.

The Watchful Eye. At almost all elections with lawyers present, the lawyers liked to stand over our shoulders to watch what we were doing. My staff sometimes felt uncomfortable. I would tell them not to be uncomfortable, because we knew what we were doing. The reason that the attorneys stood so close is because they were eager to learn. When we have a subsequent election involving the same attorneys, they rarely stood behind us – and let us do our work unimpeded. They understand that we would consult them if there were problems.

That was all well and good except for one young attorney who kept pacing back and forth in front of our table where we had two teams working. He was

Condo Board Election Revolt!

continually pounding the president's gavel in the palm of his hand. It went on for some time until I finally asked if he intended to hit me with it. With a surprised look on his face he said, "No." I said, "Then please put down the gavel and please sit down. I know you mean well. If I need you, I'll call. Besides you're blocking the membership's view of the proceedings." Members in the assembly clapped as he sat down.

Which Bank? One incumbent losing president was so upset that he left before giving the board vital information. The attorney conducting the organizational meeting was embarrassed, apologized to the board and called the loser on his cell phone to demand that he provide vital banking details to the new Board so that they could go to their bank in the morning and take control.

Not Even Close. How about the petitioner who lost by 100 votes to the next nearest candidate? He filed a complaint with the Division the next morning.

I'm in Charge. After one of my elections was over, a sweet elderly woman came up to me and asked that I step outside. I said, "What do you have in mind? I've been happily married for 50 years." She said, "Oh no. Nothing like that. There could be repercussions if they even knew I signed the petition asking you to come. But I wanted to thank you personally for giving us back our lives." "I didn't do that," I said, "You did." She replied,

Condo Board Election Revolt!

"But it wouldn't have happened had you not come. That's why I want to thank you." She then said, "I have one more question. I'm one of the new board members. Can you tell me when we take charge?" "You were in charge as soon as the election results were announced," I replied. "Oh my." she said. "Your organizational meeting to elect your new officers begins in 15 minutes," I told her. "I had better get back inside," she said, reaching over and kissing me on the cheek. She rushed away saying, "Now they are going to have to sit down, shut up and listen to us for a change. We'll see how they like it. There will be no more bullying here." After midnight, Dr. Rizzo received a half dozen calls from unit owners thanking him for our help.

Running a Run-Off. One election requiring a run-off resulted in a large number of disregarded envelopes. Despite my objection, the attending attorney decided to open one particular disregarded envelope to see how it would affect the run-off. It affected it as any disregarded ballot would have. It was irrelevant and did not change the announced election results. That attorney should attend one of those CAI courses.

Last Should be First. I conducted a fractional voting election where the fractions were recorded on the ballot. There are two things wrong with fractional voting. For example, after the election was over I could have taken half of the ballots and told the specific unit owner how he/she had voted. Second, the two candidates having

Condo Board Election Revolt!

the most votes cast for them both lost the election. We are all equal, but some are more equal than others. Needless to say fractional voting leaves much to be desired. It also does wonders for voter anonymity, the cornerstone of voting.

What Do We Do? In one election, attorneys represented both parties. Three attorneys were present – one for the association and two for the unit owners. We ended up with a tie for the last vacancy. A run-off election was required. The attorneys – who had to make the announcement – asked me about the procedure, After I explained it, they said they would be more comfortable if I presented the procedure directly to the assembly – which I did. Of course, I did not charge them for a consultation or for the service.

Stay to the End. We were often asked (indeed pressured) to stay for the organizational meeting. However, once the election was over, we no longer had any jurisdiction. Still in Miami at midnight– an hour over the time estimated to conduct the election – it was also time to return to Fort Lauderdale. Monitors had to go to work the next morning, and I had a report to write. We tried to refuse as politely as possible.

Lost Results. The morning after the election, the association lost its copy of the results of the previous evening's election. The organizational meeting was scheduled for that afternoon. The old board wanted to

Condo Board Election Revolt!

do a recount before the meeting to re-establish who won. The petitioner, who had won a seat on the board, called me and I immediately faxed him a copy of our records. The organizational meeting took place without a hitch. The petitioner called me later and said "You guys are worth every penny you charge. The check is in the mail. You've waited long enough." Obviously, the old board had custody of the election records.

So there you have it. Since I no longer have access to the records to jog my memory, that's all I can recall. Thank God, you say, enough already. I hope that these short stories lead you to understand that this was not an easy job to do. Every election was different. You never knew what you were going to run up against. Our methodology was our only constant. Using it effectively saved our bacon many times, because we had many distractions that could have created problems for us. Our disciplined approach worked, but it did not come free or easy. Considerable energy went into making it work, but work it did.

From these examples, it should be clear that the Legislature knew what it was doing when it gave the Ombudsman the responsibility to "Conduct Elections" and why so many bureaucrats are now trying to render this portion of the statute ineffective by reducing it to an observer role. When election monitors conduct an election, it works.

Chapter Eleven
Incapacitated Leader

We scheduled two elections two days apart in the Daytona Beach area in February 2006. Originally, I was scheduled to conduct both and to train three new election monitors at the same time. I couldn't make it, so Dr. Rizzo filled in for me. He drove to Daytona Beach to conduct the first election and to train the three monitors. He then returned immediately, because we both had large elections scheduled for Miami the following day, (the election the Wall Street Journal reporter was to attend.)

Driving five hundred miles in two days with back problems took its toll on Dr. Rizzo. The morning after driving back from Daytona, he woke up paralyzed from the waist down and was rushed to Jackson Memorial Hospital in Miami. The next day he underwent a ten-hour back surgery operation. The leader had fallen, and we had to fill in. Fortunately, there were no petitions to verify. It wasn't long after his surgery before the laptop computer was humming and the cell phone was ringing. Virgil was back home working from his bed.

We breathed a sigh of relief – especially because we were receiving new petitions. We kept going without missing a beat, business as usual. Virgil had been invited to meet with a task force at city hall in Miami Beach the Friday before a scheduled Saturday Town Hall meeting in Miami (at the Julius Littman North Miami Beach Performing Arts Center). He was up to it, but did not feel he should drive, so I drove him instead.

I was driving south on Collins Avenue. We reached the intersection of 92nd Street when Virgil instructed me to take a right at the intersection. I told him we had to keep going south down to 17th Street. He said he knew it, but that we were getting back on I-95 and going home. I made the right-hand turn, puzzled. He said that his medication was wearing off and that his legs were numb. He phoned the organizer to apologize for his absence. When we reached his home, Virgil refused my help and insisted on reaching his apartment under his own steam.

His condition was not improving, and he was scheduled for more surgery early May in Miami. Concerned about going under the knife for a second time, he cancelled the surgery. As medical doctor, he researched and found that he could receive laser back surgery at the Bonati Institute in Hudson, Florida – where he underwent a one-hour laser operation later that month. Several days later, he was back home somewhat improved. During this period, Virgil was on medical leave. Not that it made much difference to the Division. Sick leave was no excuse for failure to perform the duties as required while on the job.

Condo Board Election Revolt!

I've already told you about the outrageous record request demands playing out in the middle of all this. It's important to remember, because those events played a major role in Virgil's rescinded appointment. By the end of May, he felt well enough to take a short and well-deserved cruise. While he was on the cruse, indisposed and unable to defend himself, he got the ax.

When he arrived home from the cruise, he gave me a call at nine o'clock that night. I told him I was sorry to hear what happened to him. I remember asking how it felt to get sucker-punched. He replied that it wasn't quite a sucker-punch because he saw it coming, but he did not anticipate it coming that way.

He commented that I left in time and recalled telling me that he did not expect to be far behind. He was right, thirty days later for that matter. I asked him how it all came down. He said he didn't know. There was a message on his cell phone from a staff employee telling him his appointment had been rescinded. And a note to the same effect was taped to the door of his apartment. He told me that his State e-mail access had been terminated and the lock to his office had been changed. To that I replied, "In that respect we are in the same boat, you can't get at anything and I turned in all my papers and materials when I left. Now we're both blind."

Condo Board Election Revolt!

I asked if he was going to hang out a shingle and become a millionaire defending condo owners or did he plan to write a book and become famous? He said, "Neither. I'm going to be busy getting my health back." I said, "OK, then I'll write a book." That is where we left it. In mid-June he had to go back to Hudson for his third back surgery in about four months. This time the procedure lasted two hours and he ran into complications that were eventually brought under control. But sure enough, he came right back home. The difference – now he was returning to a very quiet apartment.

The laptop computer screen was blank and the cell phone was not ringing. I can imagine the empty and betrayed feeling he must have felt. I had made my decision to retire in January, 2006. In essence I had until May to completely wind down. Like Sinatra, I did it my way. In contrast, Virgil didn't have that long preparation lead time. His tenure came to a surprising and abrupt stop.

Given his medical condition, he had already instructed Representative Robaina to start looking for a replacement. However, I suspect that the abrupt ending may have taken a toll. His main concern and focus today is on his health – the right priority. Virgil is no longer my leader, but he remains a close friend. I wish to thank him on behalf of all Floridians who have extended their hands to him for help.

Chapter Twelve
Changes Needed

Early on, the Ombudsman made claims that the "rules and procedures were not only confusing, obsolete and impractical, but also ineffective, antiquated and in serious need of complete revision." The Division went ballistic. It still hasn't calmed down. But I'm here to tell you Virgil was right and, worse yet, the Division knows it.

After being involved in nearly one hundred elections over the last fifteen months for the Office of the Condominium Ombudsman as his Volunteer Chief Election Monitor, I am able to provide some specific recommendations based on personal observations. I saw first-hand how confusing, impractical, inefficient, and/or rigid statutes and rules could be – causing qualified unit owner ballots to be "Disregarded" time and again.

The Legislature should make changes to Florida Statute 718 and to Florida Administrative Code Chapter 61B that would reduce or eliminate the disenfranchisement of qualified voters on technicalities. The statutes and the rules are clear on some of the administrative requirements, silent on others, and in some instances are in need of revision where they relate to important voting issues.

Condo Board Election Revolt!

Situations such as the following should be addressed:

– Rejection of an outer envelope that contains a ballot without an inner ballot envelope.

– Disregard of a signed outer envelope that does not have a unit number, has a wrong number or the number is not legible.

– Disregard of outer envelope that contains other material along with the ballot, such as a proxy or voter certificate.

– Disregard of an inner envelope that contains one of the above in addition to the ballot.

– Disregard of a unit owner submitted ballot in an envelope other than the one mailed to him.

– Disregard if unit owner submits his own written ballot.
– Owner not allowed to vote because of voter certificate administration problems.

– Multi unit-owners, who mail multiple ballots in a single envelope, not permitted to vote the remainder of their units in person.

Condo Board Election Revolt!

Associations should not be allowed to:

– Create confusion with ballots printed in English on one side and another language on the other side;

– Provide two ballots in different languages;
– Fail to provide or run out of ballots at the election;
– Use "down level" (not current) voter lists;
– Fail to have the voter certificate book on hand;
– Fail to have a voter signature log for reference;
– Be inconsistent in acceptance and rejection of power of attorney vote recognition;
– Be inconsistent in enforcement of voter certificates for corporate units.

Statute and Rule Change Considerations:

A broad directive should be added to the statute and to the rules allowing intelligent resolution of situations where certain voting situations are not accounted for. An instruction should be added to both the statute and the rules stating: *During a regular election every attempt shall be made to legally reconcile any procedural voting mistakes made on the part of a qualified unit owner and/or the association that may cause a valid vote to be disregarded.*

Further changes should include:

– Update the qualified voter list prior to mailing the first election notice. This would ensure voting notices and materials are sent to the authorized voter. It would also

Condo Board Election Revolt!

reduce the need to disregard valid ballots. Many unit owners return the new voter certificate in the outer envelope. Some attorneys and associations have disregarded outer envelopes using the "down level" (not current) voter certificate on file, even when unit owners had instructions to include the new voter certificate with the ballot in the outer envelope.

– Allow power of attorney holders to vote in regular condominium elections. This restriction is inconsistent with the recall procedure. With power of attorney one can buy or sell a condo for someone else and can even have a doctor remove that individual from life support, but can't vote for him. As it is, many associations disregard this rule.

– Eliminate unit owner voter certificate use for regular elections. It is the easiest way for an association to prevent a legitimate owner from voting via voter certificate manipulation. They are in conflict with the undeniable right to vote. Treatment for married couples is different than for other owners in some cases, but it should not be. Same sex couples, for instance, should be afforded the same consideration. Besides, it is unclear from the description section of the statute that a voter certificate is meant to apply to business meeting issues as implied by the proxy authority text. Voter certificates should continue to be applicable for corporations and trusts where the unit ownership by a named individual is not readily identifiable.

Condo Board Election Revolt!

– Require an affidavit for Second Election Notice and possible use of a postal ledger. (The 30-cent cost per entry is worth the proof it provides.) The second notice mailing, which contains the voting materials, is more important than the First Notice. If later proven that a board failed to mail all required second notice materials, that board would then be guilty of falsifying an affidavit, raising the punishment level of the offense if one is levied later.

– Require adding the mailing list as an attachment to the second notice affidavit to clearly establish who was sent voting materials (unless a postal ledger was used).

– Require mailing the ballot to the authorized voter. The person receiving the ballot should rightly assume that if the envelope is in his name, he is on record as the authorized voter. A unit owner who is not the authorized voter should not receive voting materials in his/her name.

– Require separate return mailing for proxies and other ballots for annual voting issues. Other non-election voting issues should be kept off the election ballot and mailed separately. Currently, there is nothing to prevent them from being combined on the same ballot. If a quorum for the annual meeting is established but the 20 percent voting interest requirement is not satisfied, envelopes are not opened. Votes on the other issues before the assembly will not be counted.

Condo Board Election Revolt!

– Require voting instructions be prominently posted in BOLD letters at the election-meeting site 48 hours before the election. Bilingual postings should be considered where appropriate.

– Use separate outer envelope for each ballot submitted. A multi unit owner should be sent the number of ballots and envelopes he/she is entitled to cast. The cost excuse issue is unjustified. A multi- unit owner pays multiple assessments and is entitled to receive individual packages for each of his/her units. Providing a voting package for each unit authorized would eliminate the multi ballots contained in one outer envelope situation that sometimes result in confusion and the disregarding of ballots. It would also resolve the "having voted" check mark against all units owned by an individual, when less than all of the units have been voted for. It would clearly identify which ones had been voted for. If an owner then came to vote in person, he would be allowed to vote his remaining un-voted units without causing all kinds of confusion and running the risk of being denied the right to cast those additional ballots.

– Unsigned outer envelopes should be disregarded and the ballot not counted, but the unit owner SHOULD NOT be recorded as having voted. Ref 61B-23.0021(10)(b)

– Signature verification Ref 61B-23.0021(10)(a). The rule requires that the signature on the outer envelope be checked against a list of qualified voters. That list is usually PRINTED. On average, 50 percent of association member signatures cannot be compared to their printed name. Comparing signatures to a previously provided document such as a voter certificate may make that task more practical. Comparing a signature to a printed name is not always possible, making signature recognition a ridiculous formality 50 percent of the time. Even a handwriting expert cannot accomplish this task. He also requires a signature to compare to another signature.

– Allow a validated outer envelope containing a ballot that is not in an inner ballot envelope to be counted, rather than being "disregarded." The intent of the inner envelope is to maintain voter secrecy, not to provide a loophole for disregarding a valid ballot. Placing that ballot in a ballot envelope and sealing it does not jeopardize voter secrecy. If a voter signs his ballot, we accept it. If he does not wish to remain anonymous, we respect that. What is different here? He has already been qualified to vote. Why disregard the ballot because of an inner envelope oversight?

–Disallow printing two-sided ballots (e.g., English on one side and Spanish on the other) to further eliminate confusion and ballot rejection.

–Disallow two ballots in different language.

Condo Board Election Revolt!

–Require the one liner "vote for no more than #" on the ballot printed in Spanish also.

–Second Notice voting instructions should be required, as described in 61B23.0021(8) Currently, there is no such requirement.

–Unit owner should always be instructed not to include any materials other than the ballot envelope in outer envelope. A separate mailing is the cost of reducing the number of disregarded ballots. Other requirements may best be handled with the First Notice of Election mailing to decrease mailing cost and election confusion.

–Elimination of the 20 percent eligible voter requirement for regular condominium elections. The 20 percent requirement is an arbitrary and meaningless number that confers more power on those deciding not to vote versus those who actually vote, if apathy is high enough. This is a violation of civil and contractual rights of those wishing to vote and those wishing to run for office. Both groups are having their rights denied. It also leaves individuals in office whose term of office has expired. If only one owner voted and no one was denied the right to vote, that voter should determine the outcome of the election. There are no voter number or percentage limits in municipal elections.

Condo Board Election Revolt!

<u>Suggested Additional Mandatory Second Notice Content</u>:

– Voting instructions should clearly state that a unit owner may vote in person at the election meeting and that voting materials will be provided.

– Contain the cut-off date for submission of candidacy.

– Contain the cut-off date for submission of candidate information sheets.

– Contain information sheet restrictions explaining that each candidate has an 8.5"x11" single-sided information sheet submission restriction.

– Outer envelope should indicate a Print and a Sign space on the outer envelope, a requirement that is often violated.

– When the Ombudsman requests information, associations should be required to cooperate with the Office of the Condominium Ombudsman relative to any election related inquiry.

<u>Ombudsman Election Monitor Payment Rule Change</u> <u>Ref 61B-23.00215 (9)</u> Delete from that section the underlined text: *(9) Where a monitor is appointed who is not a Division employee, the Division will not enforce the billing and collection of amounts owed to the monitor.*

Condo Board Election Revolt!

Nothing in these rules prohibits a private monitor from requiring the association to pre-pay all or part of the reasonable fees and costs of the monitor. Reason: Fair and equitable treatment should be mandatory for everyone who performs duties for the State of Florida. At the very least, the Division should not inadvertently encourage associations not to pay volunteers, just because there is no consequence for failure to pay. No volunteer working for the State of Florida should be forced to litigate to get paid. The legislature should also provide liability protection for paid volunteer monitors, who act as volunteer agents while conducting elections.

Author's Summary

When I took on this assignment, I felt reasonably comfortable with the challenge. I was no stranger to launching operations from scratch. I was involved in several major "first" assignments in my 31-year career at IBM. Back in the early 1960s, I served as IBM's first System Manufacturing Division (SMD) Computer Assisted Instruction (CAI) manager responsible for providing online education to all the Division's manufacturing facilities. It was the other CAI.

What I was not prepared for, however, was the infighting that we would confront – and overcome – to get the job done. We were tugged upon from all sides. The Office was a political lobbying football involving those for and against condo change, with so many conflicting expectations. It was frustrating, educational and satisfying. Here is what we accomplished in that brief 15-month period:

Petitions Validated: 105
Elections Conducted: 90
Average Voter Participation: 65%
Conducted in Miami/Dade County: 42.9%
Conducted in Broward & Palm Beach Counties: 36.2%
Conducted on the Florida West Coast: 10.5%
Conducted on the Florida Central East Coast: 8.6%
Conducted in the Florida Panhandle: 1.9%

Condo Board Election Revolt!

Number of Units Served: 19,414 (Representing 1.6% of Florida's 1.2 Million Condo Owners.)
Total Petitioners: 2,912
Smallest Number of Units Served: 8
Largest Number of Units Served: 1,500
Total Candidates Who Volunteered to
Fill Vacancies: 890
Total Director Vacancies: 466

These figures demonstrate that for each of the 466 vacancies, there were on average two candidates who volunteered to fill those vacancies. This destroys the myth that you cannot find volunteers to run for office. Dr. Rizzo and I felt we had accomplished all that the legislature had mandated and more. We both went from 0 to 100 to a Full Stop in approximately 15 months.

We made it possible for the new Ombudsman to hit the ground running. We provided a solid base to improve upon. The organization now has a better understanding of the problems and yes, also the solution to those problems. That is half the battle. With added resources, she/he will have an easier time of it than we did, we hope.

The way Dr. Rizzo's appointment was rescinded left many Floridians, who were not aware of what went on backstage, with many questions and doubts about our motivation and our actions. The ending took the shine off our accomplishments.   Virgil and I have an appreciation for the disappointed feeling that must have been experienced by our GIs returning home from Vietnam, having their uniforms spat on as they arrived at LA Airport. Like them, we were in a war supported by too few in our State's bureaucracy. Virgil should have been awarded the Purple Heart and the Medal of Honor for his contributions. On the other hand, I should have been tried for desertion. I feel bad about it because he was a good boss and remains my friend.

If this book helps restore some of the luster to Virgil's accomplishments and set the record straight, it was a worthwhile enterprise. Hopefully, this book will also shed light on the huge task Dr. Rizzo was given and how much he was able to accomplish with so few resources and despite all the opposition. As Will Rogers put it, "We are all ignorant, just on different subjects." If you were ignorant of what was going on behind the scenes in our operation, you are no longer.

Condo Board Election Revolt!

Condo Board Election Revolt!

Appendix A: Florida Statute 718.12 (2d). Regular Elections Unit Owner Meetings

1. There shall be an annual meeting of the unit owners. Unless the bylaws provide otherwise, a vacancy on the board caused by the expiration of a director's term shall be filled by electing a new board member, and the election shall be by secret ballot; however, if the number of vacancies equals or exceeds the number of candidates, no election is required. If there is no provision in the bylaws for terms of the members of the board, the terms of all members of the board shall expire upon the election of their successors at the annual meeting. Any unit owner desiring to be a candidate for board membership shall comply with subparagraph 3. A person who has been convicted of any felony by any court of record in the United States and who has not had his or her right to vote restored pursuant to law in the jurisdiction of his or her residence is not eligible for board membership. The validity of an action by the board is not affected if it is later determined that a member of the board is ineligible for board membership due to having been convicted of a felony.
2. The bylaws shall provide the method of calling meetings of unit owners, including annual meetings. Written notice, which notice must include an agenda, shall be mailed, hand delivered, or electronically transmitted to each unit owner at least 14 days prior to

Condo Board Election Revolt!

the annual meeting and shall be posted in a conspicuous place on the condominium property at least 14 continuous days preceding the annual meeting. Upon notice to the unit owners, the board shall by duly adopted rule designate a specific location on the condominium property or association property upon which all notices of unit owner meetings shall be posted; however, if there is no condominium property or association property upon which notices can be posted, this requirement does not apply. In lieu of or in addition to the physical posting of notice of any meeting of the unit owners on the condominium property, the association may, by reasonable rule, adopt a procedure for conspicuously posting and repeatedly broadcasting the notice and the agenda on a closed-circuit cable television system serving the condominium association. However, if broadcast notice is used in lieu of a notice posted physically on the condominium property, the notice and agenda must be broadcast at least four times every broadcast hour of each day that a posted notice is otherwise required under this section. When broadcast notice is provided, the notice and agenda must be broadcast in a manner and for a sufficient continuous length of time so as to allow an average reader to observe the notice and read and comprehend the entire content of the notice and the agenda. Unless a unit owner waives in writing the right to receive notice of the annual meeting, such notice shall be hand delivered, mailed, or electronically transmitted to each unit owner.

Condo Board Election Revolt!

Notice for meetings and notice for all other purposes shall be mailed to each unit owner at the address last furnished to the association by the unit owner, or hand delivered to each unit owner. However, if a unit is owned by more than one person, the association shall provide notice, for meetings and all other purposes, to that one address which the developer initially identifies for that purpose and thereafter as one or more of the owners of the unit shall so advise the association in writing, or if no address is given or the owners of the unit do not agree, to the address provided on the deed of record. An officer of the association, or the manager or other person providing notice of the association meeting, shall provide an affidavit or United States Postal Service certificate of mailing, to be included in the official records of the association affirming that the notice was mailed or hand delivered, in accordance with this provision. 3. The members of the board shall be elected by written ballot or voting machine. Proxies shall in no event be used in electing the board, either in general elections or elections to fill vacancies caused by recall, resignation, or otherwise, unless otherwise provided in this chapter. Not less than 60 days before a scheduled election, the association shall mail, deliver, or electronically transmit, whether by separate association mailing or included in another association mailing, delivery, or transmission, including regularly published newsletters, to each unit owner entitled to a vote, a first notice of the date of the election. Any unit owner or

Condo Board Election Revolt!

other eligible person desiring to be a candidate for the board must give written notice to the association not less than 40 days before a scheduled election. Together with the written notice and agenda as set forth in subparagraph 2., the association shall mail, deliver, or electronically transmit a second notice of the election to all unit owners entitled to vote therein, together with a ballot which shall list all candidates. Upon request of a candidate, the association shall include an information sheet, no larger than 81/2 inches by 11 inches, which must be furnished by the candidate not less than 35 days before the election, to be included with the mailing, delivery, or transmission of the ballot, with the costs of mailing, delivery, or electronic transmission and copying to be borne by the association. The association is not liable for the contents of the information sheets prepared by the candidates. In order to reduce costs, the association may print or duplicate the information sheets on both sides of the paper. The division shall by rule establish voting procedures consistent with the provisions contained herein, including rules establishing procedures for giving notice by electronic transmission and rules providing for the secrecy of ballots. Elections shall be decided by a plurality of those ballots cast. There shall be no quorum requirement; however, at least 20 percent of the eligible voters must cast a ballot in order to have a valid election of members of the board. No unit owner shall permit any other person to vote his or her ballot, and any such ballots

Condo Board Election Revolt!

improperly cast shall be deemed invalid, provided any unit owner who violates this provision may be fined by the association in accordance with s. 718.303. A unit owner who needs assistance in casting the ballot for the reasons stated in s. 101.051 may obtain assistance in casting the ballot. The regular election shall occur on the date of the annual meeting. The provisions of this subparagraph shall not apply to timeshare condominium associations. Notwithstanding the provisions of this subparagraph, an election is not required unless more candidates file notices of intent to run or are nominated than board vacancies exist.

Condo Board Election Revolt!

Appendix B Florida Administrative Code Regular Elections 61B-23.0021 Regular Elections; Vacancies Caused by Expiration of Term, Resignations, and Death.

(1)(a) This rule apply to all regular and run-off elections conducted by a condominium association, regardless of any provision to the contrary contained in the governing documents of the association. (b) FAC Rules 61B-23.0027 and 61B-23.0028 define the method of removing board members byrecall and the procedures for filling such vacancies. This rule (61B-23.0021) does not apply to vacancies created by the recall of a board member or members. (c) To adopt different voting and election procedures for BODs an association must obtain the affirmative vote of a majority of the total voting interests even if different amendatory procedures are contained in an association's bylaws. (d) Balloting is not necessary to fill any vacancy unless there are two or more eligible candidates for that vacancy. In such a case, not later than the date of the scheduled election: 1. For a regular elections the association shall call and hold a meeting of the membership to announce the names of the new board members, or shall notify the unit owners of the names of the new board members or that one or more board positions remain unfilled, as appropriate under the circumstances. In the alternative, the announcement may be made at the annual meeting. 2. For an election

Condo Board Election Revolt!

pursuant to Section 718.112(2)(d)8., Florida Statutes, to fill a vacancy, the association shall call and hold a meeting of the membership to announce the names of the new board members or, in the alternative, shall notify the unit owners of the names of the new board members or that one or more board positions remain unfilled, as appropriate under the circumstances. (2) A regular or general election for purposes of this rule shall be an election to fill a vacancy caused by expiration of a term in office. A regular or general election shall occur at the time and place at which the annual meeting is scheduled to occur, regardless of whether a quorum is present. Other elections as may be required shall occur in conjunction with duly called meetings of the unit owners, regardless of whether a quorum is attained for the meeting. (3) A board of administration shall not create or appoint any committee for the purpose of nominating a candidate or candidates for election to the board. A board may create or appoint a search committee which shall not have the authority to nominate any candidate, but may encourage qualified persons to become candidates for the board. (4) The first notice of the date of the election, which is required to be mailed or delivered not less than 60 days before a scheduled election, must contain the name and correct mailing address of the association. (5) A unit owner or other eligible person desiring to be a candidate for the board of administration shall give written notice to the association not less than 40 days before a scheduled election. Written notice shall be effective when received by the association. Written notice shall be accomplished in accordance with one or more of the following methods: (a) By certified mail, return receipt requested, directed to the association; or (b) By personal delivery to the association; or (c) By regular U.S. mail, facsimile, telegram, or other method of delivery to the association. (6) Upon receipt by the association of any timely submitted written notice by personal delivery that a unit owner or other eligible person desires to be a candidate for the board of administration, the association shall issue a written receipt acknowledging delivery of the written notice. Candidates who timely submit a written notice by mail may wish to send the written notice by certified mail in order to obtain a written receipt. (7) Upon the timely request of a candidate as set forth in this paragraph, the association shall include, with the second notice of election described in subsection (8) below, a copy of an information sheet which may describe the candidate's background, education, and qualifications as well as other factors deemed relevant by the candidate. The information contained therein shall not exceed one side of the sheet which shall be no larger than 8 1/2 inches by 11 inches. Any candidate desiring the association to mail or personally deliver copies of an information sheet to the eligible voters must furnish the information sheet to the association not less than 35 days before the election. If two or more candidates consent in writing, the association may consolidate into a single side of a page the candidate information sheets submitted by those candidates. No association shall edit, alter, or otherwise modify the content of the information sheet. The original copy provided by the candidate shall become part of the official records of the association. (8) In accordance with the requirements of Section 718.112(2)(d), Florida Statutes. The association shall mail or deliver to the eligible voters at the addresses listed in the official records a second notice of the election, together with a ballot and any information sheets timely submitted by the candidates. The association shall mail or deliver the second notice no less than 14 days and no more than 34 days prior to the election. The second notice and accompanying documents shall not contain any communication by the board that endorses, disapproves, or otherwise comments on any candidate. Accompanying the ballot shall be an outer envelope addressed to the person or entity authorized to receive the ballots and a smaller inner envelope in which the ballot shall be placed. The exterior of the outer envelope shall indicate the name of the voter, and the unit or unit numbers being voted, and shall contain a signature space for the voter. Once the ballot is filled out, the voter shall place the completed ballot in the inner smaller envelope and seal the envelope. The inner envelope shall be placed within the outer larger envelope, and the outer envelope shall then be sealed. Each inner envelope shall contain only one

Condo Board Election Revolt!

ballot, but if a person is entitled to cast more than one ballot, the separate inner envelopes required may be enclosed within a single outer envelope. The voter shall sign the exterior of the outer envelope in the space provided for such signature. The envelope shall either be mailed or hand delivered to the association. Upon receipt by the association, no ballot may be rescinded or changed. (9) The written ballot shall indicate in alphabetical order by surname, each and every unit owner or other eligible person who desires to be a candidate for the board of administration and who gave written notice to the association not less than 40 days before a scheduled election, unless such person has, prior to the mailing of the ballot, withdrawn his candidacy in writing. No ballot shall indicate which candidates are incumbents on the board. No write-in candidates shall be permitted. No ballot shall provide a space for the signature of or any other means of identifying a voter. Except where all voting interests in a condominium are not entitled to one whole vote, (fractional voting), or where all voting interests are not entitled to vote for every candidate (class voting), all ballot forms utilized by a condominium association, whether those mailed to voters or those cast at a meeting, shall be uniform in color and appearance. In the case of fractional voting, all ballot forms utilized for each fractional vote shall be uniform in color and appearance. And in class voting situations, within each separate class of voting interests all ballot forms shall be uniform in color and appearance. (10) Envelopes containing ballots received by the association shall be retained and collected by the association and shall not be opened except in the manner and at the time provided herein. (a) Any envelopes containing ballots shall be collected by the association and shall be transported to the location of the duly called meeting of the unit owners. The association shall have available at the meeting additional blank ballots for distribution to the eligible voters who have not cast their votes. Each ballot distributed at the meeting shall be placed in an inner and outer envelope in the manner provided in subsection (8) of this rule. Each envelope and ballot shall be handled in the following manner. As the first order of business, ballots not yet cast shall be collected. The ballots and envelopes shall then be handled as stated below by an impartial committee as defined in paragraph (b) below appointed by the board. The business of the meeting may continue during this process. The signature and unit identification on the outer envelope shall be checked against a list of qualified voters, unless previously validated as provided in paragraph (b) below. Any exterior envelope not signed by the eligible voter shall be marked "Disregarded" or with words of similar import, and any ballots contained therein shall not be counted. The voters shall be checked off on the list as having voted. Then, in the presence of any unit owners in attendance, and regardless of whether a quorum is present, all inner envelopes shall be first removed from the outer envelopes and shall be placed into a receptacle. Upon the commencement of the opening of the outer envelopes, the polls shall be closed, and no more ballots shall be accepted. The inner envelopes shall then be opened and the ballots shall be removed and counted in the presence of the unit owners. Any inner envelope containing more than one ballot shall be marked "Disregarded", or with words of similar import, and any ballots contained therein shall not be counted. All envelopes and ballots, whether disregarded or not, shall be retained with the official records of the association. (b) Any association desiring to verify outer envelope information in advance of the meeting may do so as provided herein. An impartial committee designated by the board may, at a meeting noticed in the manner required for the noticing of board meetings, which shall be open to all unit owners and which shall be held on the date of the election, proceed as follows. For purposes of this rule, "impartial" shall mean a committee whose members do not include any of the following or their spouses: 1. Current board members; 2. Officers; and 3. Candidates for the board. At the committee meeting, the signature and unit identification on the outer envelope shall be checked against the list of qualified voters. The voters shall be checked off on the list as having voted. Any exterior envelope not signed by the eligible voter shall be marked "Disregarded" or with words of similar import, and any ballots contained therein shall not be counted. (c) If two or more candidates for the same position receive the same number of votes, which would result in one or more candidates not serving or serving a lesser period of time, the association shall, unless otherwise provided in the bylaws, conduct a run-off election in accordance with the procedures set forth herein. Within 7 days of the date of the election at which the tie vote occurred, the board shall mail or personally deliver to the voters, a notice of a run-off election. The only candidates eligible for the run-off election to the board position are the run-off candidates who received the tie vote at the previous election. The notice shall inform the voters of the date scheduled for the run-off election to occur, shall include a ballot conforming to the requirements of this rule, and shall include copies of any candidate information sheets previously submitted by those candidates to the association. The run-off election must be held not less than 21 days, nor more than 30 days, after the date of the election at which the tie vote occurred. (11) Any voter who requires assistance to vote by reason of blindness, disability, or inability to read or write, may request the assistance of a member of the board of administration or other unit owner to assist in casting his vote. If the election is by voting machine, any such voter, before retiring to the voting booth, may have a member of the board of administration or other unit owner or representative, without suggestion or interference, identify the specific vacancy or vacancies and the candidates for each. If a voter requests the aid of any such individual, the two shall retire to the voting booth for the purpose of casting the vote according to the voter's choice. (12) At a minimum, all voting machines shall meet the following requirements: (a) Shall secure to the voter secrecy in the act of voting; (b) Shall permit the voter to vote for as many persons and offices as he is lawfully entitled to vote for, but no more; (c) Shall correctly register or record, and accurately count all votes cast for any and all persons; (d) Shall be furnished with an electric light or proper substitute, which will give sufficient light to enable voters to read the ballots; and (e) Shall be provided with a screen, hood, or curtain which shall be made and adjusted so as to conceal the voter and his actions while voting. (13) Notices of election, notices of candidacy for election, information sheets, voting envelopes, written approval of budgets, written agreements for recall of board members, ballots, sign-in sheets, voting proxies, and all other papers relating to voting by unit owners shall be maintained as part of the official records of the association for a period of 1 year from the date of the election, vote, or meeting to which the document relates.

APPENDIX C: Condominium Ombudsman Section of Statute 718.5011 Ombudsman; Appointment; Administration.

(1) There is created an Office of the Condominium Ombudsman, to be located for administrative purposes within the Division of Florida Land Sales, Condominiums, and Mobile Homes. The functions of the office shall be funded by the Division of Florida Land Sales, Condominiums, and Mobile Homes Trust Fund. The ombudsman shall be a bureau chief of the division, and the office shall be set within the division in the same manner as any other bureau is staffed and funded. (2) The Governor shall appoint the ombudsman. The ombudsman must be an attorney admitted to practice before the Florida Supreme Court and shall serve at the pleasure of the Governor. A vacancy in the office shall be filled in the same manner as the original appointment. An officer or full-time employee of the ombudsman's office may not actively engage in any other business or profession; serve as the representative of any political party, executive committee, or other governing body of a political party; serve as an executive, officer, or employee of a political party; receive remuneration for activities on behalf of any candidate for public office; or engage in soliciting votes or other activities on behalf of a candidate for public office. The ombudsman or any employee of his or her office may not become a candidate for election to

Condo Board Election Revolt!

public office unless he or she first resigns from his or her office or employment. History.--s. 6, ch. 2004-345. 718.5012 Ombudsman; powers and duties.--The ombudsman shall have the powers that are necessary to carry out the duties of his or her office, including the following specific powers: (1) To have access to and use of all files and records of the division. (2) To employ professional and clerical staff as necessary for the efficient operation of the office. (3) To prepare and issue reports and recommendations to the Governor, the department, the division, the Advisory Council on Condominiums, the President of the Senate, and the Speaker of the House of Representatives on any matter or subject within the jurisdiction of the division. The ombudsman shall make recommendations he or she deems appropriate for legislation relative to division procedures, rules, jurisdiction, personnel, and functions. (4) To act as liaison between the division, unit owners, boards of directors, board members, community association managers, and other affected parties. The ombudsman shall develop policies and procedures to assist unit owners, boards of directors, board members, community association managers, and other affected parties to understand their rights and responsibilities as set forth in this chapter and the condominium documents governing their respective association. The ombudsman shall coordinate and assist in the preparation and adoption of educational and reference material, and shall endeavor to coordinate with private or volunteer providers of these services, so that the availability of these resources is made known to the largest possible audience. (5) To monitor and review procedures and disputes concerning condominium elections or meetings, including, but not limited to, recommending that the division pursue enforcement action in any manner where there is reasonable cause to believe that election misconduct has occurred. (6) To make recommendations to the division for changes in rules and procedures for the filing, investigation, and resolution of complaints filed by unit owners, associations, and managers. (7) To provide resources to assist members of boards of directors and officers of associations to carry out their powers and duties consistent with this chapter, division rules, and the condominium documents governing the association. (8) To encourage and facilitate voluntary meetings with and between unit owners, boards of directors, board members, community association managers, and other affected parties when the meetings may assist in resolving a dispute within a community association before a person submits a dispute for a formal or administrative remedy. It is the intent of the Legislature that the ombudsman act as a neutral resource for both the rights and responsibilities of unit owners, associations, and board members. (9) Fifteen percent of the total voting interests in a condominium association, or six unit owners, whichever is greater, may petition the ombudsman to appoint an election monitor to attend the annual meeting of the unit owners and conduct the election of directors. The ombudsman shall appoint a division employee, a person or persons specializing in condominium election monitoring, or an attorney licensed to practice in this state as the election monitor. All costs associated with the election monitoring process shall be paid by the association. The division shall adopt a rule establishing procedures for the appointment of election monitors and the scope and extent of the monitor's role in the election process. History.--ss. 7, 36, ch. 2004-345. 718.5014 Ombudsman location.--The ombudsman shall maintain his or her principal office in Leon County on the premises of the division or, if suitable space cannot be provided there, at another place convenient to the offices of the division which will enable the ombudsman to expeditiously carry out the duties and functions of his or her office. The ombudsman may establish branch offices elsewhere in the state upon the concurrence of the Governor.

APPENDIX D: Statute 61B-23.00215 Ombudsman; Election Monitoring; Monitor's Role; Scope and Extent.

(I) Fifteen percent of the total voting interests entitled to vote at the annual meeting of unit owners for the election of directors. or the owners of six units entitled to vote at the annual meeting of unit owners for the election of directors, whichever number is greater, may petition the ombudsman for the appointment of an election monitor to attend the annual meeting of unit owners for the election of directors and conduct the election of directors. No monitor shall he appointed for a special election, an interim election. a run-off election, an election to fill vacancies caused by a recall of one or more board members, or any election other than the annual meeting of unit owners for the election of directors.(2)(a) Form of petition. In order to file a petition for the appointment of art election monitor, a unit owner   must complete DBPR FORM CO 6000-9, PETITION FOR APPOINTMENT OF ELECTION MONITOR, incorporated by reference and effective 8-7-05, available by contacting the Division of Florida Land Sales, Condominiums, and Mobile Homes, Northwood Centre. 1940, North Monroe. Tallahassee, Florida 32399-1030. or shall use a substantial equivalent of the form which shall contain the following information. The form must, as applicable:1. State that the purpose of the petition is to seek signatures for the

Condo Board Election Revolt!

appointment of an election monitor by the ombudsman for the annual meeting of unit owners for the election of directors;2. Contain a signature space for authorized unit owners or voting interests to sign and must provide a space for those signing the petition to provide his or her name:3.Identify his or her unit number:4.Supply the date that each unit owner signed the petition;5. Provide the name of an individual who is authorized to represent the unit owners petitioning for the appointment of an election monitor, along with the mailing address, telephone number, fax number, and email address of the representative;6. Indicate that if a monitor is appointed, the association and all its members shall be obligated to pay the costs and fees of the monitor; and7.State the total number of voting interests in the association,8. Briefly state the basis for having an election monitor appointed (optional).9.State the date, place, and time of the election.(b) Only the signatures of those persons who are unit owners of record shall be counted in the calculation to determine whether the minimum number of votes have been cast in favor of requesting the appointment of a monitor.(3) Time to file. The petition for appointment of an election monitor must he filed with the ombudsman not less than 14 days in advance of a planned election to provide sufficient time to process the petition, provide for verification of the signatures, and appoint a monitor.(4) Once the ombudsman has received a timely filed petition for appointment of an election monitor, the ombudsman shall examine the petition to ensure that all required information is provided and that a sufficient number of voting interests have signed the petition.(a)   If the petition is deficient, the ombudsman shall provide the petitioners with notice of the deficiencies, and petitioners will have 5 calendar days from receipt of such notice to timely correct the petition, or if the deficiencies cannot he corrected, the petition shall be denied and the materials shall be returned to the unit owners petitioning for appointment of an election monitor.

(b) Within 5 calendar days of the determination that a petition is complete and sufficient, the ombudsman shall provide a copy of the petition to the association by certified mail, along with a notice that a petition for appointment of election monitor has been filed with the ombudsman. Where the determination that a petition is complete and sufficient is made within 5 days of a scheduled election, the ombudsman shall immediately provide a copy of the petition to the association upon making such determination of completeness.(5) Once a petition has been found to be adequate, the ombudsman shall appoint an election monitor as provided by the provisions of Section 718.5012(9), Florida Statutes, and this rule. Any appointment of a division employee shall he subject to the approval of the division director.(6)

The appointed monitor shall review any documents provided by the petitioners or by the

Condo Board Election Revolt!

association in advance of the scheduled election and shall attend and conduct the election in person.(7) The monitor shall conduct the election, but where a division employee is appointed as monitor, the employee shall not provide direct advice or suggestions to the association or to individual owners in the course of the election. Each monitor shall submit a report regarding the election to the ombudsman, and to the parties, within 14 days following the date the election is concluded.(8) Where a division employee has been approved to be appointed as the election monitor, the division shall prepare an itemized statement of costs and expenses and shall submit the statement and a request for reimbursement to the association along with the monitor's report. The association shall have 30 days in which to reimburse the division. It shall he considered a violation of this rule for an association not to timely reimburse the division for all costs and expenses associated with the election monitoring process.(9) Where a monitor is appointed who is not a division employee, the division will not enforce the billing and collection of amounts owed to the monitor. Nothing in these rules prohibits a private monitor from requiring the association to pre-pay all or part of the reasonable fees and costs of the monitor. Specific Authority 718.5012(9) FS. Law Implemented 718.1255, 7I8.5012(9) FS.

Condo Board Election Revolt!

APPENDIX E: Chapter 61B-21 Condo Resolution Guidelines for Unit Owner Controlled Associations.

Definitions and Purpose. 61B-21.002
Educational Resolution. 61B-21.003
Enforcement Resolution and Civil Penalties. 61B-21.001

Definitions and Purpose.

(1) Definitions. For the purposes of this rule chapter, the following definitions shall apply: (a) "Accepted Complaint" means a complaint received by the division containing sufficient documentation and addressing a subject within the jurisdiction of the division, pursuant to Section 718.501(1), F.S. (b) "Affirmative or corrective action" means putting remedial procedures in place to ensure that the violation does not recur, making any injured person whole as to the harm suffered in relation to the violation, or taking any other appropriate measures to redress the harm caused. (c) "Alleged repeated violation" means any accepted complaint for the same or substantially similar recurring conduct received by the division within two years from the resolution of a previous complaint regarding that conduct. (d) "Association," for purposes of these guidelines, shall have the same meaning as stated in Section 718.103(2), F.S. (e) "Bad check" means any worthless check, draft, or order of payment identified under Section 68.065, F.S. (2) Purpose. The purpose of

Condo Board Election Revolt!

the resolution guidelines is to implement the division's responsibility to ensure compliance with the provisions of Chapter 718, F.S., and the division's administrative rules. The division recognizes that unit owner controlled associations are comprised of volunteer members who, in most circumstances, are lay people without specialized knowledge of the complex statutory and administrative rule structure of Chapter 718, F.S. Based upon this understanding, the division, as set forth in these rules, will first and foremost attempt to seek statutory and rule compliance through an educational resolution. For repeated statutory or rule violations, where the violations have not been corrected or otherwise resolved by the association, the division will seek statutory or rule compliance through an enforcement resolution. The guidelines are also intended to implement the division's statutory authority to give reasonable and meaningful notice to persons regulated by Chapter 718, F.S., and the administrative rules of the range of penalties that normally will be imposed, if an enforcement resolution is taken by the division. Finally, the rules are intended, pursuant to statutory mandate, to distinguish between minor and major violations based upon the potential harm that the violation may cause. (3) These penalty guidelines are promulgated pursuant to the division's authority in Section 718.501(1)(d), (f), and (k), F.S. This rule chapter does not preclude the division from imposing affirmative or corrective action pursuant to Section

Condo Board Election Revolt!

718.501(1)(d)2., F.S. Nothing in this rule chapter shall limit the ability of the division to informally dispose of administrative actions or complaints by stipulation, settlement agreement, or consent order. Rules 61B-21.001, and 61B-21.002, and 61B-21.003, F.A.C., are necessary to explicate the division's education and enforcement policy. This rule chapter is not intended to cover, or be applied to, willful and knowing violations of Chapter 718, F.S., or the administrative rules by an officer or association board member, pursuant to Section 718.501(1)(d)4., F.S. Such violations shall be strictly governed by the provisions of Section 718.501(1)(d)4., F.S. This rule chapter is not intended to cover, or be applied to, violations of Chapter 718, F.S., or the administrative rules by a condominium developer as defined by Section 718.103(15), F.S. Such violations shall be strictly governed by the provisions of Rules 61B-20.004, 61B-20.005, and 61B-20.006, F.A.C., and Section 718.301(5), F.S. Specific Authority 718.501(1)(d)4.,(f) FS. Law Implemented 718.501(1)(d)4.,(k) FS. HistoryûNew 6-4-98. 61B-21.002 Educational Resolution. (1) The educational resolution process, as detailed in this rule chapter, is only applicable to unit owner controlled associations. (2) Alleged Initial Violation. An initial accepted complaint, directed at an association and involving a possible violation identified as minor in these guidelines, will be resolved as follows: The division will review the matter and will contact the association board by letter or telephone regarding the complaint. The division will provide educational materials or guidance to the association board to assist it with addressing the subject matter of the complaint and provide the association with the opportunity to respond. The division will notify the complainant of the educational resolution and the division's complaint file will be closed.(3) Alleged Repeated Violations. A subsequent accepted complaint, directed at the same association involving a possible violation identified as minor in these guidelines, will be resolved as follows: If based on the complaint, the division has reasonable cause to believe that a statutory or rule violation may have occurred, a Warning Letter will be sent to the association. The Warning Letter will give the association a reasonable period of time in which to address, correct, or dispute the violation. The Warning Letter will identify the violation, and provide a contact telephone number and an investigator's name so that the association may contact the division for educational assistance or an educational conference in obtaining compliance. However, it is solely the responsibility of the association to take action, when applicable, to achieve statutory or rule compliance. Failure to respond to a Warning Letter, or take affirmative or corrective action as requested by the division, will lead to further investigation. The Warning Letter shall not be considered final agency action. The division will notify the complainant of the edcuational resolution, or if applicable, alternative dispute resolution options. (4) Alleged Major Violations. An initial accepted complaint, directed at an association and involving a possible violation identified as major in these guidelines, will be resolved as follows: If based on the complaint, the division has reasonable cause to believe that a statutory or rule violation may have occurred, a Warning Letter will be sent to the association. The Warning Letter will give the association a reasonable period of time in which to address, correct, or dispute the violation. The Warning Letter will identify the violation, and provide a contact telephone number and an investigator's name so that the association may contact the division for educational assistance or an educational conference in obtaining compliance. However, it is solely the responsibility of the association to take action, when applicable, to achieve statutory or rule compliance. Failure to respond to a Warning Letter, or take affirmative or corrective action as requested by the division, will lead to further investigation. The Warning Letter shall not be considered final agency action. The division will notify the complainant of the educational resolution, or if applicable, alternative dispute resolution options.Specific Authority 718.501(1)(d)4.,(f) FS. Law Implemented 718.501(1)(d)4.,(k) FS. HistoryûNew 6-4-98. 61B-21.003 Enforcement Resolution and Civil Penalties. (1) The division will seek compliance through an enforcement resolution for repeated minor or major violations, or for the failure to correct or address a violation or provide unit owner redress as requested by the division. These guidelines list aggravating and mitigating factors that will reduce or increase the listed penalty amounts within the specified range and those circumstances that justify a departure from the range. No aggravating factors will be applied to increase a penalty for a single violation above the statutory maximum of $5,000. The guidelines in this rule chapter are based upon a single count violation of each provision listed. Multiple counts of the violated provision or a combination of the listed violations will be added together to determine an overall total penalty. Nothing in this rule chapter shall limit the ability of the division to informally dispose of administrative actions orcomplaints by stipulation, settlement agreement, or consent order. (2) General Provisions. (a) Rule Not All-Inclusive. This rule chapter contains illustrative violations. It does not, and is not intended to, encompass all possible violations of statute or division rule that might be committed by an association. The absence of any violation from this rule chapter shall in no way be construed to indicate that the violation does not cause substantial harm or is not subject to a penalty. In any instance where the violation is not listed in this rule chapter, the penalty will be determined by consideration of: 1. The closest analogous violation, if any, that is listed in this rule chapter; and 2. The mitigating or aggravating factors listed in this rule chapter. (b) Violations Included. This rule chapter

Condo Board Election Revolt!

applies to all statutory and rule violations subject to a penalty authorized by Chapter 718, F.S.(c) Rule Establishes Norm. These guidelines do not supersede the division's authority to order an association to cease and desist from any unlawful practice, or order other affirmative action in situations where the imposition of administrative penalties is not adequate. For example, notwithstanding the specification of relatively smaller penalties for particular violations, the division will suspend the imposition of a penalty and impose other remedies where aggravating or mitigating factors warrant it. If an enforcement resolution is utilized, the total penalty to be assessed shall be calculated according to these guidelines or $100, whichever amount is greater. (d) Description of Violations. Although the violations in Rule 61B-21.003, F.A.C., include specific references to statutes and administrative rules, the violations are described in general language and are not necessarily stated in the same language that would be used to formally allege a violation in a specific case. If any statutory or rule citation in Rule 61B-21.003, F.A.C., is changed, then the use of the previous statutory citation will not invalidate this rule chapter. (3) Aggravating and Mitigating Factors. The division will consider aggravating and mitigating factors in determining penalties for violations listed in this rule chapter. The factors are not necessarily listed in order of importance, and they shall be applied against each single count of the listed violation. (a) Aggravating Factors: 1. Filing or causing to be filed any materially incorrect document in response to any division request or subpoena. 2. Financial loss to parties or persons affected by the violation. 3. Financial gain to parties or persons who perpetrated the violation. 4. The disciplinary history of the association, including such action resulting in an enforcement resolution as detailed in Rule 61B-21.003, F.A.C., or Section 718.501, F.S.5. The violation caused substantial harm, or has the potential to cause substantial harm, to condominium residents or other persons. 6. Undue delay in initiating or completing, or failure to take, affirmative or corrective action after the association received the division's written notification of the violation. 7. The violation had occurred for a long period of time. 8. The violation was repeated within a short period of time. 9. The association impeded the division's investigation or authority. 10. The investigation involved the issuance of a notice to show cause or other proceeding. (b) Mitigating Factors: 1. Whether current members of the association board have sought and received educational training, other than information provided pursuant to Rule 61B-21.002, F.A.C., on the requirements of Chapter 718, F.S., within the past two years. 2. Reliance on written professional or expert counsel and advice. 3. Acts of God or nature. 4. The violation caused no harm to condominium residents or other persons. 5. The association took affirmative or corrective action before it received the division's written notification of the violation. 6. The association expeditiously took affirmative or corrective action after it received the division's written notification of the violation. 7. The association cooperated with the division during the investigation. 8. The investigation was concluded through consent proceedings. (4) The provisions of this rule chapter shall not be construed so as to prohibit or limit any other civil or criminal prosecution that may be brought. (5) The imposition of a penalty does not preclude the division from imposing additional sanctions or remedies provided under Chapter 718, F.S. (6) In addition to the penalties established in this rule chapter, the division reserves the right to seek to recover any other costs, penalties, attorney's fees, court costs, service fees, collection costs, and damages allowed by law. Additionally, the division reserves the right to seek to recover any costs, penalties, attorney's fees, court costs, service fees, collection costs, and damages imposed by law if an association submits a bad check to the division. (7) Penalties. (a) Minor Violations. The following violations shall be considered minor due to their lower potential for consumer harm. If an enforcement resolution is utilized, the division shall impose a civil penalty between $1 and $5, per unit, for each minor violation. The penalty will be assessed beginning with the middle of the specified range and adjusted either up or down based upon any accepted aggravating or mitigating factors. An occurrence of six or more aggravating factors or five or more mitigating

Condo Board Election Revolt!

factors will result in a penalty being assessed outside of the specified range. The total penalty to be assessed shall be calculated according to these guidelines or $100, whichever amount is greater. Finally, in no event shall a penalty of more than $2,500 be imposed for a single violation. The following are identified as minor violations: Category Statute or Rule Cite Description of Conduct/Violation Elections 718.112(2)(d)3., FS. Improper nomination procedures in election. 61B-23.0021(3), FAC Elections 718.112(2)(d)3., FS. Including a candidate who did not provide timely 61B-23.0021(5), FAC. notice of candidacy. Elections 61B-23.0021(6), FAC. Failure to provide candidate a receipt for written notice of intent to be a candidate. Elections 61B-23.0021(8), (10), FAC. Counting ballots not cast in inner and outer envelopes. Failure to provide space for name and signature on outer envelope. Elections 61B-23.0021(10)(c), FAC. Failure to timely hold run-off election. (b) Major Violations. The following violations shall be considered major due to their increased potential for consumer harm. If an enforcement resolution is utilized, the penalty will be assessed beginning with the middle of the specified range and adjusted either up or down based upon any accepted aggravating or mitigating factors. An occurrence of six or more aggravating factors or five or more mitigating factors will result in a penalty being assessed outside of the specified range. The total penalty to be assessed shall be calculated according to

Condo Board Election Revolt!

these guidelines or $100, whichever amount is greater. Finally, in no event shall a penalty of more than $5,000 be imposed for a single violation. The penalties are set forth in categories 1 and 2, for each violation as follows: Category 1: $6 û $10 per unit. Category 2: $12 û $20 per unit. Category Statute or Rule Cite Description of Conduct/Violation Suggested Penalty Elections 718.112(2)(d), FS. Failure to hold election. 2 61B-23.0021(2), FAC Elections 718.112(2)(d)3., FS. Failure to use ballots or voting machines. 2 Elections 718.112(2)(d)3., FS. Failure to provide, or timely provide, first 1 61B-23.0021(4), FAC. notice of election. Elections 718.112(2)(d)3., FS. Failure to provide, or timely provide, second 1 61B-23.0021(7),(8), FAC. notice of election or omitting materials such as ballots, envelopes, and candidate information sheets. Elections 718.112(2)(d)3., FS. Failure to include all timely submitted 1 61B-23.0021(9), FAC. names of eligible candidates on the ballot. Elections 61B-23.0021(10)(a),(b), FAC. Counting ineligible ballots. Not counting 1 Specific Authority 718.501(1)(f), 718.501(1)(d)4. FS. Law Implemented 718.501(1)(d)4., 718.501(1)(k) FS. HistoryûNew 6-4-98. ballots in the presence of unit owners. Elections 61B-23.0021(10)(c), FAC. Failure to hold run-off election. 2. Providing lower level of reporting for 2

Condo Board Election Revolt!

APPENDIX F: Advisory Council On Condominiums 718.50151 Advisory Council; Membership Functions.

(1)   There is created the Advisory Council on Condominiums. The council shall consist of seven appointed members. Two members shall be appointed by the President of the Senate, two members shall be appointed by the Speaker of the House of Representatives, and three members shall be appointed by the Governor. At least one member that is appointed by the Governor shall represent timeshare condominiums. Members shall be appointed to 2-year terms; however, one of the persons initially appointed by the Governor, by the President of the Senate, and by the Speaker of the House of Representatives shall be appointed to a 1-year term. The director of the division shall serve as an ex officio nonvoting member. The Legislature intends that the persons appointed represent a cross-section of persons interested in condominium issues. The council shall be located within the division for administrative purposes. Members of the council shall serve without compensation but are entitled to receive per diem and travel expenses pursuant to s. 112.061 while on official business. (2) The functions of the advisory council shall be to: (a) Receive, from the public, input regarding issues of concern with respect to condominiums and recommendations for changes in the condominium law.

Condo Board Election Revolt!

The issues that the council shall consider include, but are not limited to, the rights and responsibilities of the unit owners in relation to the rights and responsibilities of the association. (b) Review, evaluate, and advise the division concerning revisions and adoption of rules affecting condominiums. (c) Recommend improvements, if needed, in the education programs offered by the division. (3) The council may elect a chair and vice chair and such other officers as it may deem advisable. The council shall meet at the call of its chair, at the request of a majority of its membership, at the request of the division, or at such times as it may prescribe. A majority of the members of the council shall constitute a quorum. Council action may be taken by vote of a majority of the voting members who are present at a meeting where there is a quorum.

APPENDIX G: Division Of Florida Land Sales, Condominiums, And Mobile Homes 718.501   Powers and duties of Division of Florida Land Sales, Condominiums, and Mobile Homes.

(1) The Division of Florida Land Sales, Condominiums, and Mobile Homes of the Department of Business and Professional Regulation, referred to as the "division" in this part, in addition to other powers and duties prescribed by chapter 498, has the power to enforce and ensure compliance with the provisions of this chapter and rules promulgated pursuant hereto relating to the development, construction, sale, lease, ownership, operation, and management of residential condominium units. In performing its duties, the division has the following powers and duties: (a) The division may make necessary public or private investigations within or outside this state to determine whether any person has violated this chapter or any rule or order hereunder, to aid in the enforcement of this chapter, or to aid in the adoption of rules or forms hereunder. (b) The division may require or permit any person to file a statement in writing, under oath or otherwise, as the division determines, as to the facts and circumstances concerning a matter to be investigated. (c) For the purpose of any investigation under this chapter, the division director or any officer or employee designated by the division director may administer

Condo Board Election Revolt!

oaths or affirmations, subpoena witnesses and compel their attendance, take evidence, and require the production of any matter which is relevant to the investigation, including the existence, description, nature, custody, condition, and location of any books, documents, or other tangible things and the identity and location of persons having knowledge of relevant facts or any other matter reasonably calculated to lead to the discovery of material evidence. Upon the failure by a person to obey a subpoena or to answer questions propounded by the investigating officer and upon reasonable notice to all persons affected thereby, the division may apply to the circuit court for an order compelling compliance. (d)   Notwithstanding any remedies available to unit owners and associations, if the division has reasonable cause to believe that a violation of any provision of this chapter or rule promulgated pursuant hereto has occurred, the division may institute enforcement proceedings in its own name against any developer, association, officer, or member of the board of administration, or its assignees or agents, as follows: 1. The division may permit a person whose conduct or actions may be under investigation to waive formal proceedings and enter into a consent proceeding whereby orders, rules, or letters of censure or warning, whether formal or informal, may be entered against the person. 2. The division may issue an order requiring the developer, association, officer, or member of the board of administration, or its assignees or agents, to cease and desist from the unlawful practice and take such affirmative action as in the judgment of the division will carry out the purposes of this chapter. Such affirmative action may include, but is not limited to, an order requiring a developer to pay moneys determined to be owed to a condominium association.

3. The division may bring an action in circuit court on behalf of a class of unit owners, lessees, or purchasers for declaratory relief, injunctive relief, or restitution. 4. The division may impose a civil penalty against a developer or association, or its assignee or agent, for any violation of this chapter or a rule promulgated pursuant hereto. The division may impose a civil penalty individually against any officer or board member who willfully and knowingly violates a provision of this chapter, a rule adopted pursuant hereto, or a final order of the division. The term "willfully and knowingly" means that the division informed the officer or board member that his or her action or intended action violates this chapter, a rule adopted under this chapter, or a final order of the division and that the officer or board member refused to comply with the requirements of this chapter, a rule adopted under this chapter, or a final order of the division. The division, prior to initiating formal agency action under chapter 120, shall afford the officer or board member an opportunity to voluntarily comply with this chapter, a rule adopted under this chapter, or a final order of the division. An officer or board

member who complies within 10 days is not subject to a civil penalty. A penalty may be imposed on the basis of each day of continuing violation, but in no event shall the penalty for any offense exceed $5,000. By January 1, 1998, the division shall adopt, by rule, penalty guidelines applicable to possible violations or to categories of violations of this chapter or rules adopted by the division. The guidelines must specify a meaningful range of civil penalties for each such violation of the statute and rules and must be based upon the harm caused by the violation, the repetition of the violation, and upon such other factors deemed relevant by the division. For example, the division may consider whether the violations were committed by a developer or owner-controlled association, the size of the association, and other factors. The guidelines must designate the possible mitigating or aggravating circumstances that justify a departure from the range of penalties provided by the rules. It is the legislative intent that minor violations be distinguished from those which endanger the health, safety, or welfare of the condominium residents or other persons and that such guidelines provide reasonable and meaningful notice to the public of likely penalties that may be imposed for proscribed conduct. This subsection does not limit the ability of the division to informally dispose of administrative actions or complaints by stipulation, agreed settlement, or consent order. All amounts collected shall be deposited with the Chief Financial

Condo Board Election Revolt!

Officer to the credit of the Division of Florida Land Sales, Condominiums, and Mobile Homes Trust Fund. If a developer fails to pay the civil penalty, the division shall thereupon issue an order directing that such developer cease and desist from further operation until such time as the civil penalty is paid or may pursue enforcement of the penalty in a court of competent jurisdiction. If an association fails to pay the civil penalty, the division shall thereupon pursue enforcement in a court of competent jurisdiction, and the order imposing the civil penalty or the cease and desist order will not become effective until 20 days after the date of such order. Any action commenced by the division shall be brought in the county in which the division has its executive offices or in the county where the violation occurred. (e) The division is authorized to prepare and disseminate a prospectus and other information to assist prospective owners, purchasers, lessees, and developers of residential condominiums in assessing the rights, privileges, and duties pertaining thereto. (f) The division has authority to adopt rules pursuant to ss. 120.536(1) and 120.54 to implement and enforce the provisions of this chapter. (g) The division shall establish procedures for providing notice to an association when the division is considering the issuance of a declaratory statement with respect to the declaration of condominium or any related document governing in such condominium community. (h) The division shall furnish each association which pays the

Condo Board Election Revolt!

fees required by paragraph (2)(a) a copy of this act, subsequent changes to this act on an annual basis, an amended version of this act as it becomes available from the Secretary of State's office on a biennial basis, and the rules promulgated pursuant thereto on an annual basis. (i) The division shall annually provide each association with a summary of declaratory statements and formal legal opinions relating to the operations of condominiums which were rendered by the division during the previous year. (j) The division shall provide training programs for condominium association board members and unit owners. (k) The division shall maintain a toll-free telephone number accessible to condominium unit owners. (l) The division shall develop a program to certify both volunteer and paid mediators to provide mediation of condominium disputes. The division shall provide, upon request, a list of such mediators to any association, unit owner, or other participant in arbitration proceedings under s. 718.1255 requesting a copy of the list. The division shall include on the list of volunteer mediators only the names of persons who have received at least 20 hours of training in mediation techniques or who have mediated at least 20 disputes. In order to become initially certified by the division, paid mediators must be certified by the Supreme Court to mediate court cases in either county or circuit courts. However, the division may adopt, by rule, additional factors for the certification of paid mediators, which factors must be related to experience,

Condo Board Election Revolt!

education, or background. Any person initially certified as a paid mediator by the division must, in order to continue to be certified, comply with the factors or requirements imposed by rules adopted by the division. (m) When a complaint is made, the division shall conduct its inquiry with due regard to the interests of the affected parties. Within 30 days after receipt of a complaint, the division shall acknowledge the complaint in writing and notify the complainant whether the complaint is within the jurisdiction of the division and whether additional information is needed by the division from the complainant. The division shall conduct its investigation and shall, within 90 days after receipt of the original complaint or of timely requested additional information, take action upon the complaint. However, the failure to complete the investigation within 90 days does not prevent the division from continuing the investigation, accepting or considering evidence obtained or received after 90 days, or taking administrative action if reasonable cause exists to believe that a violation of this chapter or a rule of the division has occurred. If an investigation is not completed within the time limits established in this paragraph, the division shall, on a monthly basis, notify the complainant in writing of the status of the investigation. When reporting its action to the complainant, the division shall inform the complainant of any right to a hearing pursuant to ss. 120.569 and 120.57. (2)(a) Effective January 1, 1992, each

Condo Board Election Revolt!

condominium association which operates more than two units shall pay to the division an annual fee in the amount of $4 for each residential unit in condominiums operated by the association. If the fee is not paid by March 1, then the association shall be assessed a penalty of 10 percent of the amount due, and the association will not have standing to maintain or defend any action in the courts of this state until the amount due, plus any penalty, is paid. (b) All fees shall be deposited in the Division of Florida Land Sales, Condominiums, and Mobile Homes Trust Fund as provided by law.

Condo Board Election Revolt!

INDEX*

* This index was created with **TExtract**™ - a product of Texyz Indexing
Software at **www.texyz.com**

170

Condo Board Election Revolt!

Condo Board Election Revolt!

multiple   31, 54
petition   66
Unopened outer envelopes
60
Unsigned outer envelopes
48, 99, 118

V
Vacancies   30, 37, 97,
107, 124
Volunteer Chief Election
Monitor   1, 3, 113
Volunteers   2, 3, 8, 21,
24, 26, 29, 53, 54, 56-60,
70, 74, 80, 81, 86, 97,
122, 124
Vote   31-33, 36, 37, 45,
47, 48, 61, 62, 96, 99-103,
105, 114, 116-121
  counting   37
  qualified   58
  valid   56, 115
Voter
  anonymity   107
  authorized   31, 115, 117
  list   99
    authorized   55, 58
    qualified   48, 115
  secrecy   119
Voting   47, 99, 107, 115,
116
  envelopes   48, 94, 99
  fractional   106, 107
  instructions   19, 36,
101, 118, 121

www.ingramcontent.com/pod-product-compliance
Lightning Source LLC
Chambersburg PA
CBHW020245290326
41930CB00038B/357

* 9 7 8 0 9 7 9 2 3 3 3 9 5 *